The Financial Legacy

The Financial Legacy

Honoring Dad's Prosperity

RAFEAL MECHLORE

WSM Publisher

CONTENTS

CONTENT	vii
COPYRIGHT	xv

1	Chapter	1
2	Chapter	11
3	Chapter	23
4	Chapter	43
5	Chapter	63

CONTENT

The Financial Legacy: Honoring Dad's Prosperity

RAFEAL MECHLOR

TABLE OF CONTENT

Introduction

Setting the stage: Introduce the concept of a financial legacy and its significance in our lives.

Personal connection: Share a personal story of the author's relationship with their father and the impact of his financial success.

Chapter 1: Discovering Dad's Financial Journey

Early life and upbringing: Explore the factors that influenced Dad's financial mindset and his journey towards prosperity.

Lessons learned: Highlight the valuable financial lessons imparted by Dad and their impact on the author's life.

Overcoming challenges: Discuss the obstacles Dad faced and the strategies he employed to overcome them.

Chapter 2: Unveiling Dad's Financial Strategies

Saving and investing: Examine Dad's approach to saving money and his investment strategies.

Creating multiple streams of income: Explore the various ventures Dad pursued to generate wealth.

Building a financial support system: Discuss how Dad surrounded himself with trusted advisors and mentors to enhance his financial decision-making.

Chapter 3: Preserving and Growing the Financial Legacy

Estate planning: Explain the importance of estate planning and the steps Dad took to ensure a smooth transition of wealth.

Continuity in family business: Explore how Dad groomed the next generation to carry forward his entrepreneurial endeavors.

Philanthropic endeavors: Highlight Dad's charitable contributions and the values instilled in the author regarding giving back to society.

Chapter 4: Lessons for Future Generations

Instilling financial literacy: Discuss the importance of teaching children about money management and share Dad's strategies for imparting financial literacy.

Nurturing the entrepreneurial spirit: Explore Dad's encouragement of entrepreneurship and how it shaped the author's mindset.

Balancing wealth and values: Discuss the role of values in managing and preserving a financial legacy.

Chapter 5: Honoring Dad's Prosperity

Emotional inheritance: Highlight the non-financial aspects of Dad's legacy, such as values, work ethic, and family bonds.

Honoring Dad's values: Share personal anecdotes and stories that exemplify the values Dad instilled and how the author continues to honor them.

Paying it forward: Discuss the author's commitment to passing on Dad's financial legacy to future generations.

Conclusion

1. Reflecting on the journey: Summarize the key lessons learned from Dad's financial legacy.
2. Inspiring readers: Encourage readers to reflect on their own financial legacies and the steps they can take to honor and preserve them.

3. Final thoughts: Express gratitude for Dad's prosperity and the impact it has had on the author's life.

Introduction

One of the most crucial ideas in personal finance is the notion of leaving a financial legacy. It encompasses all theories and practices that have an impact on someone's financial condition both now and in the future, affecting future generations. As a result of our lifetime efforts, our financial legacy bears the weight of our values, goals, and successes.

The significance of recognizing a father's accomplishments and the legacy he leaves behind is discussed in this essay. It looks at the numerous dimensions of a financial legacy, including the creation and preservation of wealth as well as the sharing of knowledge, ideas, and a sense of responsibility. It is a reflection on the significance of the monetary choices made by our ancestors and the invaluable lessons we learn from them.

A parent leaves behind much more than simply material wealth when it comes to finances. It includes a strong sense of stewardship, empowerment, and accountability. By appreciating and honoring our forefathers' affluence, we get insight into the ideas that underpinned their prosperity and the teachings they wanted to convey. By teaching, defending, and communicating, we may carry on their legacy and ensure the prosperity of present and future generations. Let's embark on this journey to learn more about and show appreciation for the financial legacy that our forefathers have left behind.

One of the most crucial ideas in personal finance is the notion of leaving a financial legacy. It encompasses all theories and practices that have an impact on someone's financial condition both now and in the future, affecting future generations. As a result of our lifetime efforts, our financial legacy bears the weight of our values, goals, and successes.

In this paragraph, we examine the crucial subject of honoring a father's accomplishments and the legacy he leaves behind. We look at the various components of a financial legacy, from the creation and upkeep of money to the communication of knowledge, ideas, and a sense of responsibility. It is a reflection on the significance of the monetary choices made by our ancestors and the invaluable lessons we learn from them.

The degree of financial literacy a person possesses is heavily influenced by their education. It provides us with the knowledge and tools we require to successfully negotiate the challenging world of personal finance. Our fathers, who served as our first financial role models, had a big impact on how we perceived wealth and money. Our financial journey is built on the suggestions and lessons they provided. We look at the importance of a father's wisdom and the need to instill a mindset that is long-term and abundance-focused.

Building wealth is a journey that requires tenacity, concentration, and foresight. Our fathers frequently envision a prosperous future for their families, themselves, and their dreams. We examine the strategies they employ to accumulate and diversify their wealth. We delve into the principles of efficient wealth creation, covering everything from understanding risk management to investing in various asset types. We also examine the role that flexibility plays in managing rapidly changing economic conditions.

Estate planning is crucial to preserve a family's wealth and leave a lasting legacy. Our fathers understand the importance of creating a comprehensive estate plan that protects assets and distributes them in accordance with their wishes. Among other estate planning instruments, we discuss powers of attorney, trusts, and wills. We also look into ways to lessen any issues and tax consequences.

Prudent investment is a crucial component of creating and keeping wealth. Our fathers employ various financial strategies to increase benefits while lowering risks. We delve into the foundations of prudent investing, like asset allocation and portfolio diversification. We also talk about the idea of coordinating financial options.

through the sponsorship of ecological and socially conscious enterprises, with personal aspirations and societal impact.

It takes transferring knowledge and concepts from one generation to the next in order to maintain a financial legacy. The promotion of financial literacy and accountability depends on having frank and open discussions about money. We talk about the importance of father-son talks when our fathers share their wisdom, financial know-how, and information. These conversations pave the way for the next generation to make moral decisions and continue the heritage.

The ability to inculcate financial literacy in children at a young age is a gift from our fathers. We examine approaches for teaching kids about prudent money management, saving, budgeting, and spending. By promoting an entrepreneurial spirit and financial creativity, our fathers equip us with the skills we need to properly manage the financial opportunities and challenges that lie ahead.

Our fathers' financial heritage comprises both the capacity to contribute to society and individual prosperity. We might have a lasting effect through generosity on problems that align with our family's interests and values. We talk about the need of promoting a donating and civic-minded culture. In order to ensure that the money we donate to charity has a genuine and long-lasting impact on the globe, we also consider effective charitable giving strategies.

Inheriting wealth comes with a certain set of responsibilities and challenges. The financial legacies left by our fathers come with a psychological and emotional cost that affects social interactions and overall welfare. We discuss the potential difficulties of inheriting wealth and the importance of doing it with respect and humility. Finding a balance between money prosperity and general pleasure becomes a key goal as we commemorate our dads' achievements.

The financial legacy of a father is proof of their success and of the values they uphold. Beyond tangible wealth, it contains a strong sense of accountability, stewardship, and empowerment. We gain understanding of the ideas that

underlay the prosperity of our ancestors and the principles they strove to impart via the appreciation and respect of their wealth. By teaching, defending, and communicating, we may carry on their legacy and ensure the prosperity of present and future generations. Let's embark on this journey to learn more about and show appreciation for the financial legacy that our forefathers have left behind.

CONTENT

COPYRIGHT

Copyright © 2023 by RAFEAL MECHLORE

All rights reserved. No part of this book may be reproduced in any manner whatsoever without written permission except in the case of brief quotations embodied in critical articles and reviews.

WSM Publisher 2023

Chapter 1

Chapter 1
Discovering Dad's Financial Journey

I found a dusty old box in the attic on a warm summer's afternoon. I cautiously removed the lid, revealing a treasure trove of lost memories, and my curiosity was piqued. I discovered a group of documents that will eventually reveal the tale of my dad's financial journey among the pictures and souvenirs.

The papers showed a young guy just beginning his adult life, one with goals and ambitions. Dad worked as a delivery boy for a nearby grocery store as his first job. He was able to save every dollar he could because to his perseverance and diligence. I was able to deduce from the faded receipts and bank statements that he scrupulously kept track of his expenses while always trying to make ends meet.

I discovered documents as I combed through the box further, showing a change in Dad's financial course. He seemed to have taken a risk and launched his own modest business. The records, which included descriptions of both successes and failures, demonstrated the highs and lows of entrepreneurship. It was clear that he put his entire being into his endeavor because he was passionate about improving the future of our family.

I discovered a battered notebook among the pile of papers that was jam-packed with figures and scribbles. Dad kept excellent track of his investments, which demonstrated his commitment to achieving financial success. In an effort to assure a better future, he had dabbled in the world of stocks, bonds, and real estate. I learned from reading his notes that he had put many hours into his study, analysis, and decision-making.

A sequence of handwritten letters addressed to me that I found as I dug deeper into the box would forever change how I understood my dad's financial path. He shared his knowledge and experiences in these touching letters, imparting priceless lessons on money and life. He highlighted the value of prudent investment, saving, and living within one's means. These letters served as a testament to his affection for and desire to support his family financially.

The financial records also revealed the costs Dad paid to reach his objectives. He had chosen to save money for our future needs and education instead of spending it on extravagant vacations, expensive automobiles, and other luxuries. It became clear that his deep-seated desire to make life better for us guided every choice he made.

I couldn't help but feel awe and thankfulness for my dad's financial journey as I closed the box. His commitment, tenacity, and undying faith in a better tomorrow had defined the history of our family. I made a commitment to continue his legacy, make wise financial decisions, and impart the value of financial literacy to future generations after being inspired by his example.

My opinion of my dad changed when I learned about his financial history from that dingy old box. He developed into more than simply a father figure; he also served as an inspiration and a role model. He had demonstrated to me through his ups and downs, successes and failures, that financial success is not just determined by wealth but also by the will to succeed and the capacity to teach others important lessons.

I couldn't help but think back on the lessons I had learnt as I came to a conclusion about my investigation of Dad's financial journey. Money is a tool that, when used effectively, can alter lives, empower families, and leave a lasting legacy. It is not just a way to acquire material stuff.

It was now my duty to carry the torch that Dad had ignited for us in terms of achieving financial security, making sure that his efforts had not been in vain.

I put the box aside with a fresh feeling of purpose, prepared to start my own financial adventure. I pushed forward, anxious to make my mark and create a better future for myself and others who would come after me, armed with the knowledge and insights I had learned from my father.

1.1 Early life and upbringing: Examine the elements that shaped Dad's financial outlook and his path to success.

It is crucial to go into my dad's early life and upbringing in order to comprehend his financial philosophy and his path to riches. He was nurtured by parents who instilled in him strong ideals that would impact his relationship with money while growing up in a modest home.

Dad frequently recalled his youth and related tales of thrift and resourcefulness. Because of his parents' financial struggles, he had a very different outlook on money. He gained an understanding of the significance of financial security and the importance of hard work from watching his parents work long hours to support the family.

Dad's financial outlook was significantly influenced by his education. He was committed to doing well in school even with the minimal resources available. He was able to continue his study through scholarships and part-time work, arming himself with skills that would come in handy in his future undertakings. He became quite interested in finance and investments around this time.

Dad was lucky to have mentors and role models that helped him along his financial journey throughout his life. These people were vital in forming his perspective and giving him the skills he needed to successfully traverse the difficult world of finance, whether it was a professor who shared insights on investing or a successful entrepreneur who gave insightful business advise.

Dad's financial thinking was significantly influenced by his cultural upbringing as well. He grew up in a culture that valued responsibility for money management along with discipline, hard effort, and long-term planning. He recognized the need of prioritizing family necessities, setting aside money for the future, and preserving financial security.

Beyond the influence of outside events, Dad's own motivation and perseverance drove him onward. He had an entrepreneurial spirit from an early age and was constantly looking for ways to improve his life and the lives of those he cared about. On his path to financial success, his desire and willingness to take measured risks set him apart.

Dad's route was no different from any other in terms of obstacles and hurdles, as no financial journey is without them. He overcame several obstacles on the way, from personal losses to economic downturns. But it was his perseverance and unflinching faith in his skills that enabled him to get through these challenges and carry on working toward his objectives.

Dad's financial perspective changed as he obtained more information and experience. He shifted his attention from stability and survival to expansion and prosperity. He started to view money as a tool for creating possibilities, supporting his family, and leaving a lasting legacy rather than merely a way to fulfill fundamental requirements.

Dad never lost sight of the principles that had been taught in him from an early age during the course of his journey. Integrity, honesty, and sound financial management were important to him. His decisions were influenced by these beliefs, which made sure that his success was based on moral behavior.

Dad's financial path provided him with priceless knowledge that he was anxious to impart to subsequent generations. He supported the value of financial literacy and the necessity of starting early to teach kids about money. He intended to enable others to make wise financial decisions and build profitable futures through his own experiences.

Early experiences and upbringing of my father greatly influenced his financial outlook and path to success. His achievement was a result of the morals he was raised with, the education he received, and the impact of mentors and role models. He paved the way for himself and his family by perseverance, hard effort, and uncompromising adherence to his ideals.

I feel motivated to carry on his legacy as I think back on his journey. I'll make an effort to pass on to future generations the same principles, information, and tenacity that helped my father. His experience serves as a reminder that our perspective, motivation, and fortitude are just as important to our financial success as any other external factors.

1.2 Lessons learned: Emphasize Dad's invaluable financial advice and how it affected the author's life.

Dad stressed the value of saving as one of his first and most important financial teachings. He instilled in me the habit of saving a portion of my income or allowance since I was a small child. He emphasized that saving created possibilities for future chances and financial security in addition to serving as a safety net for crises.

Saving seemed like a hassle when I was younger, but as I got older, I realized how important it was. Dad demonstrated to me how regular, tiny savings account deposits might add up over time. He would frequently share with me tales of how his own strict saving practices had allowed him to invest in his business endeavors and follow ambitions that would not have been possible otherwise.

I developed a sense of financial responsibility because to this early lesson in saving. I discovered the importance of controlling my spending and setting up money for vital objectives like school, travel, and future investments. I am thankful for this lesson now as I look back on my life because it laid a solid basis for my financial journey.

The art of budgeting was another important financial lesson that Dad instilled in me. He would sit down with me and go over the household budget, explaining how each dollar was divided up between different costs, such as bills and groceries as well as investments and savings. He underlined the necessity to make thoughtful decisions about our expenditures and to live within our means.

I gained the ability to prioritize my spending and make thoughtful judgments about how to use my funds by creating a budget. Dad urged me to make realistic spending plans for all elements of my life, including entertainment, clothing, and leisure pursuits. This discipline not only prevented me from overspending but also improved my ability to save money for the future.

This lesson became increasingly more important as I approached maturity and faced financial independence. While many of my peers struggled with debt and excessive spending, budgeting skills gave me confidence. It made it possible for me to save money for the future while still living well and avoiding the demands of consumerism.

The importance of investments was one of Dad's most memorable lessons. He would frequently discuss how investing our money correctly may make it work for us. He exposed me to several investing alternatives, from the stock market to real estate, and described the possible risks and advantages of each.

He demonstrated to me from his personal experiences how investment may generate passive income and amass wealth over time. He highlighted the need for investing diversification to reduce risk, and he showed me the value of taking a long-term view while making financial decisions.

I started looking at investing options myself as I became more confident in my financial expertise. Dad would carefully walk me through it, urging me to take measured chances and learn from both wins and disappointments. I now have a diversified investment portfolio that offers financial stability and room for growth as a result of his advice.

My father's entrepreneurial path motivated me to pursue it myself. He demonstrated to me the link between taking chances and following one's passions and both financial success and personal joy. My understanding of the value of perseverance and adaptation in the face of uncertainty has been greatly influenced by his experiences of overcoming obstacles in his commercial endeavors.

Dad was the strongest supporter of my new business when I first launched it. He was always prepared to provide a helping hand, encourage me, and offer crucial advise. His business enthusiasm and encouragement gave me the courage to chase my dreams and put in a lot of effort to meet my financial objectives.

Beyond material prosperity, Dad instilled in me the value of communal service. He thought that wealth should be distributed fairly and that it was our duty to do our part to ensure the welfare of others. He demonstrated to me the satisfaction and delight that come from giving, whether it was through charitable contributions, volunteering, or aiding friends and family members who were in need.

I learned from this experience that achieving financial success also involves having a positive influence on other people's lives in addition to your own. This lesson has stayed with me throughout my life, and I actively look for chances to volunteer and donate to organizations that share my ideals.

The importance of financial education was one of the greatest things my father ever gave me. He pushed me to study books, go to seminars, and research materials to learn more about personal finance and investing. He held that information was essential to making wise financial decisions and avoiding traps.

This focus on financial literacy has had a significant influence on my life. I can now confidently navigate the complicated financial world and take charge of my financial destiny thanks to it. Knowing that learning is a lifetime endeavor, I continue to give learning a high priority and look for ways to increase my financial literacy.

Dad's lessons have had a significant impact on how I've handled money. They have helped me develop a feeling of responsibility, discipline, and long-term planning. I've been able to establish financial stability and make progress toward my goals through saving, setting aside money for investments, budgeting, and embracing entrepreneurship.

Furthermore, these lessons go beyond just achieving financial success. They helped me develop a strong sense of honesty, generosity, and fortitude. They have equipped me with the knowledge and skills I need to successfully navigate the dynamic world of personal finance.

I am appreciative of Dad's enduring legacy as I reflect on the influence of his lessons. His sound financial advice still serves as my mentor, and I make it a point to impart these priceless teachings to next generations in order to uphold his legacy.

1.3 Overcoming difficulties: Talk about the difficulties Dad encountered and the methods he used to get through them.

Dad faced many obstacles and setbacks on his path to financial success. These challenges, which included both personal and economic suffering, put his resiliency and resolve to the test. But he never let these difficulties define him or stop him from achieving his objectives. Instead, he used a variety of tactics to get through these challenges and carry on with his progress.

Dad used adaptation as one of his main coping mechanisms. He was aware that the financial landscape was always changing and that adaptability to these changes was essential for long-term success. He would evaluate the situation, spot fresh chances, and modify his company plans as necessary during economic downturns.

Dad's capacity for adaptation helped him get through challenging times and locate additional sources of income. Whether he was broadening his

He was always eager to accept change and take advantage of new opportunities, whether it involved commercial opportunities or researching new industries.

Dad understood the value of having a strong support system during trying times. He surrounded himself with people who had his entrepreneurial drive, were prepared to offer advice and help, and who shared his values. In order to gain knowledge from seasoned experts, he sought out mentors and joined business networks.

Dad found vital information and guidance that assisted him in overcoming obstacles thanks to these contacts. He was not hesitant to seek for assistance when necessary and was aware that working together in a team may achieve greater success than going it alone.

Adopting a growth mentality was one of Dad's most important strategies. He didn't see setbacks as failures, but rather as chances for growth and learning. He had the confidence that obstacles were only transitory and that he could get through them by being persistent and having a good outlook.

Dad was open-minded when it came to problems, looking for creative solutions and continuously picking up new skills. He didn't let failures define him or hold him back. Instead, he turned them into stepping stones that helped him advance and succeed even more.

Dad had a tremendous toolkit for conquering obstacles: knowledge. He was aware of the value of maintaining knowledge and constantly learning new things. He would spend time and energy during challenging times learning about new industries, developing trends, and cutting-edge tactics.

Dad sought to learn the skills required to tackle challenges through books, seminars, and networking activities. He thought that having knowledge and flexibility offered him a competitive edge and enabled him to face obstacles with assurance.

Perhaps Dad's resilience was his most notable attribute. Despite hardship, he resisted giving up or conceding defeat. He addressed problems with unwavering resolve and the conviction that a solution was just around the corner.

Dad was able to reorganize, reevaluate his plans, and come back even after suffering substantial setbacks. He recognized that obstacles were an inevitable part of the path and that persistence through hardship was frequently necessary for success.

Dad also used a great tactic called a positive outlook. He had a strong belief in the benefits of positive thinking and how it affected his capacity to overcome obstacles. Even in the most trying situations, he would keep a good attitude and concentrate on the chances rather than the challenges that lay ahead.

Dad would frequently remind himself and people around him that difficulties were only transitory and could be overcome with the proper outlook and tenacity. He overcame obstacles and persevered through trying times because of his optimism and everlasting faith in his ability.

Dad's strategy for conquering obstacles was based on perseverance and hard effort. He was aware that success took persistent effort and dedication and did not come easily. He would roll up his sleeves and do the work required to discover a solution even when confronted with challenges that seemed insurmountable.

Dad had an exceptional work ethic, and to get the job done, he frequently went above and beyond what was required. He was a firm believer in the virtue of tenacity and the notion that effort will eventually bear fruit.

Dad's journey served as an example of the strength in conquering obstacles. He was able to overcome challenges and succeed financially by being adaptable, creating a support system, adopting a growth mindset, pursuing knowledge, being resilient, cultivating a positive mindset, persevering, and working hard.

Anyone having difficulties in their own financial journey can learn a lot from his ideas. They serve as a reminder that setbacks are temporary and that, with the correct attitude, willpower, and strategy, we are capable of overcoming even the most difficult challenges and coming out stronger on the other side. Dad's tale is a ray of light and inspiration, showing that success is achievable despite the difficulties we encounter.

2

Chapter

CHAPTER 2
Unveiling Dad's Financial Strategies

This in-depth manual attempts to explore the money management techniques used by fathers all over the world to accumulate wealth, ensure financial security, and prepare the way for a wealthy future. This article examines many strategies and methods that have been successful in managing personal finances, from setting a budget and saving money to investing and retirement planning. People can learn helpful insights and useful advice to improve their own financial well-being and accomplish their long-term goals by learning about these tactics.

Real-world examples, advice, and professional insights will be interwoven throughout the piece to give readers helpful direction and motivation. People can better grasp how to manage their personal finances, accumulate wealth, and safeguard their future by learning about dad's financial tactics. Remember that anyone can use these tactics to become financially successful, regardless of gender.

We enter into a realm of wisdom as we set out on the road of revealing dad's financial tactics; this insight contains the key to accumulating riches and securing our future. In this thorough study, we examine the strategies used by fathers all across the world to efficiently manage their own finances. Anyone seeking financial security can learn a great deal from their experiences, perceptions, and helpful advice.

Dad's financial tactics are built around the idea of having certain financial goals. Dads are aware of the value of imagining their ideal financial future and creating a plan to get there. They methodically establish budgets, keeping track of every dime that enters and leaves their lives. They create a safety net to weather any storm that may come their way with discipline and dedication by saving aside money for emergencies.

Dads are aware that saving is a way of life, not just a decision. They use a variety of saving techniques, including automating their funds, haggling over bills and spending, and refraining from impulsive purchases. Additionally, they are aware of the weight of debt and use clever debt management strategies to pay off debts quickly, freeing up more money for investing and saving. They establish a solid financial foundation by cultivating a positive connection with money.

Dads are aware that investing is an essential part of building money. They diversify their portfolios by being knowledgeable about various investment vehicles in an effort to reduce risks. Their investment choices are guided by a long-term perspective, which enables them to weather market swings and generate steady returns over time. They carefully investigate risks to reduce them, and when necessary, they seek the advice of financial professionals.

A major component of dad's financial tactics is retirement preparation. They recognize the value of early preparation and make the most of employer-sponsored plans and retirement accounts to increase their savings. Additionally, they use catch-up techniques as necessary to make sure they are on pace to meet their retirement objectives. Dads create the groundwork for a relaxing and worry-free retirement by diligently planning.

Dads who comprehend tax rules and regulations can successfully negotiate the complex world of taxes. They carefully maximize deductions and credits by utilizing tax-advantaged accounts. When necessary, they consult a specialist, making sure to maximize their tax positions. Dads can decrease their tax liability and keep more of their hard-earned money by using appropriate tax preparation tactics.

Dads are aware of the value of safeguarding their loved ones and their possessions. To ensure their families' financial security in the event of unanticipated situations, they obtain life insurance. Their well-being is protected by health and disability insurance, and their priceless things are protected by property and casualty insurance. Dads build a safety net that guards their financial security by purchasing extensive insurance coverage.

One of dad's financial strategies is estate planning. They write wills to make sure their preferences are followed and their possessions are allocated the way they want. They create trusts to safeguard their assets and lower estate taxes. Additional measures parents take to make sure their loved ones are taken care of and their financial legacies are safeguarded include naming beneficiaries and establishing power of attorney.

Dads are aware that a gift like financial knowledge might influence their kids' futures. From an early age, they teach their kids the value of money and the importance of saving, budgeting, and investing. Dads can encourage their kids to develop sound financial practices that will benefit them throughout their life by setting a good example.

Dads are resilient and adaptable enough to deal with economic ups and downs. They modify their investment approaches to handle turbulence, seeing chances even in trying circumstances. Dads can continue to accumulate money and safeguard their financial security by keeping themselves informed, remaining adaptable, and accepting change.

The efficiency of dad's financial tactics is demonstrated by instances from daily life and success stories. These motivating tales teach us important lessons and shed light on the road to financial success. These inspirational tales lead us in the direction of our own financial objectives. Dads' knowledge and techniques for handling their

personal finances serve as a road map for success. We obtain a deeper grasp of how to accumulate wealth, establish financial security, and safeguard our future by revealing these tactics. The first step toward achieving financial well-being is to identify clear goals,

smart planning and prudent investing. We can all follow in the footsteps of dads and fulfill our financial ambitions if we put in the necessary effort, practice good discipline, and make a commitment to continuing learning.

2.1 Saving and investing: Consider Dad's methods for both saving and investing.

Dad has always used saving and investing as the cornerstones of his strategy for handling his money and assuring a wealthy future. Dad's dedication to saving begins with a thrifty attitude that he develops over time. Knowing the importance of every dollar he has worked so hard to achieve, he makes an effort to reduce wasteful spending while giving priority to necessities. Dad lives by the maxim "A penny saved is a penny earned," and it permeates every aspect of his life. He makes sure that every dollar goes as far as it can by meticulously checking pricing at the grocery store and looking for special offers and specials on large purchases.

Dad approaches saving by establishing specific financial objectives. He is aware of the value of setting clear, attainable goals, whether they be for retirement, paying for his children's school, or saving for a down payment on a home. He creates a thorough budget that breaks down his earnings, outgoing costs, and savings contributions with these objectives in mind. He can monitor his progress toward his goals thanks to this strict budgeting procedure and make necessary adjustments.

The establishment of an emergency fund is another crucial component of Dad's saving strategy. He is aware that because life is erratic, unforeseen financial difficulties can appear at any time. Dad saves a portion of his income into an easily accessible savings account to protect himself and his family from these concerns. This emergency fund serves as a safety net, offering monetary security in the event of a job loss, unexpected medical costs, or other unforeseen events.

Dad also strongly believes in living within his means. He refrains from taking on excessive amounts of debt and only does so for necessary expenditures like a house or a car. By effectively handling his debt, he keeps himself out of a vicious cycle of debt and prevents the dwindling of his savings due to interest payments.

While Dad's commitment to saving is a good start, he is also aware that saving is not the only way to amass long-term wealth. He adopts the idea of investing to maximize his financial potential. Dad considers investment to be a crucial tool for increasing his money and reaching his long-term financial objectives.

Dad's investment strategy is based on caution and due diligence. He thoroughly investigates several investment alternatives in an effort to comprehend the possible risks and benefits of each. By distributing his capital among a variety of assets, including stocks, bonds, real estate, and mutual funds, he diversifies his investment portfolio. He is able to reduce risks and avoid becoming overexposed to any one asset class thanks to this diversified approach.

Dad also uses diversification and a long-term investment plan. He understands that the best returns frequently go to those who stay engaged for the long term, therefore he is patient and steadfast in his commitment to his assets. He steers clear of acting rashly based on momentary market swings and concentrates on the core characteristics of his investments.

When necessary, Dad also consults with financial professionals for help. Although he actively manages his finances, he recognizes the need of expert guidance in intricate financial concerns. To acquire a new perspective, learn about any blind spots, and make sure that his investing approach is in line with his overall financial objectives, he interacts with financial experts.

The power of compound interest is one of Dad's guiding beliefs when it comes to investing. He begins early since he is aware that the compounding effect can cause even modest investments to rise substantially over time. He uses the power of compounding to quicken the process of accumulating wealth by routinely reinvested his investment profits and donations.

Dad also has a good eye for spotting potential financial opportunities. He keeps up with industrial advancements, market trends, and monetary situations. He is able to identify prospective growth opportunities and make wise investment selections because to his proactive approach. Dad isn't averse to stepping outside of his comfort zone to take advantage of potential chances, whether it's investing in cutting-edge technologies, developing markets, or sustainable businesses.

Dad's investment approach includes regular reviews and rebalancing as another important component. He reviews his investment portfolio on a regular basis to make sure it is in line with his risk tolerance, financial objectives, and market conditions. To keep the appropriate balance between risk and return, he rebalances his portfolio as needed by changing the distribution of his investments. Dad has a disciplined, patient, and long-term perspective when it comes to saving and investing. His dedication to being economical, setting goals, and budgeting provides the foundation for accumulating money through saves. Dad maximizes his financial potential by combining wise investment choices, diversification, and the impact of compound interest. Anyone looking to achieve financial security and build a wealthy future can learn a lot from his strategy.

2.2 Establishing several streams of income: Examine the various business endeavors Dad undertook to amass riches.

One important component of Dad's strategy for building wealth and reaching financial freedom is developing several streams of income. Dad is aware that depending only on one source of money can be dangerous and restrict his ability to progress. Dad has investigated and pursued numerous businesses to develop many sources of income in an effort to reduce this risk and boost his earning potential. Dad has been able to diversify his income and create a stronger financial base thanks to this thorough investigation of several income streams. We'll look into a few of Dad's business endeavors in this part to see how they helped him become wealthy.

Business ventures and entrepreneurship

Dad started and now runs his own company as a result of his entrepreneurial spirit. Dad welcomes the opportunities that come with entrepreneurship, whether it is a tiny local business or a larger-scale endeavor. To build profitable enterprises, he spots market gaps, creates novel concepts, and takes measured risks. Dad makes money through his entrepreneurial enterprises from a variety of sources, like product sales, service fees, or rental revenue.

Investments in real estate

Dad is aware of the potential for real estate to be a successful financial strategy. He makes investments in residential or commercial real estate and buys assets that can produce rental revenue. To make wise investment decisions, Dad carefully assesses market conditions, does extensive research, and when necessary, consults with experts. Dad uses the power of real estate to generate a consistent flow of passive income that improves his entire financial situation.

Dividend Payouts:

Dad is a proponent of stock investments that produce dividends. He chooses respectable businesses with a history of timely dividend payments with consideration. Dad generates a consistent cash flow by investing in these stocks and receiving recurring dividend income. Dad can benefit from his investments thanks to dividend income without necessarily selling the underlying assets.

Freelancing and Side Businesses:

Dad appreciates the value of using his skills and talents to make extra money. He looks into other side businesses and freelancing possibilities that fit with his interests and areas of skill. Dad uses his abilities to generate additional income by consulting, freelancing in his area of competence, or pursuing passion projects. Along with supplementing his main source of income, these side jobs give him the freedom and flexibility to pursue his interests.

Intellectual property and royalties

Dad is aware of the potential revenue sources connected to intellectual property. Dad makes money by receiving royalties from all of his creative pursuits, whether they involve publishing a book, creating music, or developing digital material. He makes use of his abilities and experience to develop intellectual properties that, over time, produce passive revenue. Dad diversifies his income and opens the door to long-term earnings by making the most of his special talents.

Investing and lending between individuals:

To make money, Dad looks into alternative investing channels like crowdfunding and peer-to-peer lending. He is aware of the benefits of expanding his investment portfolio's diversification beyond conventional channels. Dad invests a portion of his money after carefully analyzing the risks involved and performing due diligence on potential lenders or investment opportunities. Dad gains interest or returns through these alternative investment platforms, which add to his other sources of income.

Online companies and online shopping:

Dad is aware of the enormous prospects the internet era offers. He establishes online enterprises or engages in e-commerce endeavors to take advantage of the potential of the internet. Dad makes money by tapping into the enormous online market by selling goods through an online store, dropshipping, affiliate marketing, or by producing digital goods and courses. Dad now has more ways to make money because to the adaptability, scalability, and worldwide reach of online businesses.

Income from Rentals on Assets:

Dad looks into alternative options outside real estate that can produce rental income. These resources can include everything from automobiles and machinery to warehouses and parking lots. Dad appreciates the benefits of utilizing his assets to produce passive income. He makes the most of the potential of his assets by renting them out, adding another source of income.

Internet marketing:

Dad looks into network marketing opportunities as a way to get more money. He conducts in-depth research on respectable businesses that offer top-notch goods and services and have a solid track record. Dad is aware that network marketing success demands work, commitment, and developing a strong network of clients and distributors. Dad utilizes a business approach that has the ability for both active and passive revenue by adopting network marketing.

Franchising and licensing

Dad looks into the possibility of franchise or licensing options. He thinks about forming collaborations with well-known brands or companies that let him use their intellectual property, name recognition, or operational frameworks. Dad can benefit financially from the goodwill and commercial success of already-established companies while retaining some of his independence thanks to licensing or franchising arrangements. Dad's desire to pursue different revenue streams demonstrates his entrepreneurial spirit, openness to exploring new possibilities, and strategic thinking. Dad reduces risk, increases earning potential, and builds a strong financial base by diversifying his sources of income. His forays into entrepreneurship, real estate, investments, royalties, online enterprises, and other sources of income-generation show his dedication to monetary growth and the development of lasting riches. Anyone looking to diversify their sources of income and achieve financial freedom can learn a lot from Dad's strategy.

2.3 Establishing a financial support network: Talk about how Dad surrounded himself with dependable mentors and counselors to improve his financial judgment.

Dad's strategy for improving his financial decision-making includes the critical step of creating a financial support network. Dad is aware that he cannot successfully negotiate the complexity of personal finance on his alone and that consulting with mentors and trusted advisors can have a big impact on his financial performance. Dad develops his financial savvy and learns important insights into making wise and strategic financial decisions by surrounding himself with qualified experts and seasoned mentors. We will look into Dad's financial support system and the advantages it has provided him in this section.

Financial Consultants:

Dad is aware of the importance of consulting experts when it comes to handling his cash. He hires the help of reputable financial experts who are knowledgeable in things like estate preparation, tax planning, retirement planning, and investment planning. These consultants give Dad unbiased advice, assist him in comprehending difficult financial ideas, and help him develop tailored plans to reach his financial objectives. Dad is able to make decisions that are in line with his overall financial goals by consulting regularly with his financial experts.

Accountants:

Dad is aware of the significance of keeping proper financial records and abiding by tax laws. He enlists the aid of competent accountants with a focus on personal finance. Dad gets assistance from these experts with tax planning, tax return preparation, and making sure he gets the most out of his credits and deductions. Dad works with accountants to make sure that his financial affairs are in order, lowering the possibility of expensive mistakes or audits.

legal specialists

Dad is aware of the value of legal knowledge in securing his assets, reducing liabilities, and creating strong legal frameworks. He seeks advice from lawyers with expertise in corporate law, asset protection, and estate planning. These experts help Dad draft wills, trusts, and other legal papers to protect his assets from any liabilities and to ensure that his preferences are carried out regarding their distribution. Dad works with lawyers because it provides him piece of mind and protects his financial security.

Mentors and Business Advisors:

Dad consults mentors and seasoned business gurus for assistance in his entrepreneurial ventures. These people can provide invaluable insights into business plans, industry trends, and expansion prospects because they have in-depth knowledge of and practical experience in a variety of industries. Dad uses their knowledge to improve his business strategies, spot potential problems, and come to wise judgments. Dad receives access to a network of mentors who may offer advice and support throughout his entrepreneurial path by developing ties with successful business owners.

Investment specialists:

Dad seeks the advice of financial experts to maximize his investment portfolio since he is aware of the complexity of the investment landscape. He seeks the counsel of portfolio managers, financial planners, or stockbrokers who have specialized knowledge in asset allocation, investment opportunities, and risk control. These experts do in-depth research, keep an eye on market developments, and help Dad make investing decisions that are in line with his risk appetite and financial objectives. Dad works closely with investing experts so he can benefit from their specialized expertise and make wise investment decisions.

Support groups and peer networks:

Dad is aware of the value of interacting with people who have similar values and aims in terms of money. He takes an active part in peer networks, support groups, or financial communities where he may share ideas, get counsel from others, and absorb their experiences. Dad can talk about money issues on these platforms, learn from others' experiences, and receive insight into the collective knowledge. Dad gains more financial knowledge and is inspired to stick to his financial goals by being a member of a group that is encouraging.

Friends and family:

Dad understands the value of asking his loved ones for help and guidance. He shares his financial goals and seeks their advice in frank discussions about personal finance with his family and close friends. These dependable people offer a different viewpoint, moral support, and might share their personal experiences and lessons acquired. Dad respects their viewpoints and makes well-rounded decisions that take both personal and financial factors into account.

Dad's focus on creating a solid financial foundation shows his dedication to making wise financial decisions and realizing his full financial potential. Dad develops his financial savvy, learns insightful lessons, and steers clear of potential traps by surrounding himself with dependable advisors, mentors, and helpful networks. Dad improves his ability to make decisions, ensures compliance with regulations, protects his assets, and receives guidance in pursuing his financial goals through collaboration with financial advisors, accountants, legal professionals, business advisors, investment professionals, peer networks, and loved ones. Anyone looking to improve their own financial decision-making and achieve long-term financial success can learn a lot from Dad's dedication to creating a strong financial support system.

CHAPTER 3
Preserving and Growing the Financial Legacy

For people and families seeking long-term prosperity and stability, maintaining and expanding their financial legacies is a vital priority. It is vital to establish policies that protect wealth and encourage its long-term growth in this dynamic economic environment. This in-depth study explores the numerous aspects of maintaining and expanding a financial legacy. Goal-setting, efficient financial planning, investment methods, risk management, and estate planning are all covered in detail. Individuals can pave the road for a healthy financial future and leave a lasting legacy for future generations by comprehending and putting these fundamental ideas into practice.

Building and preserving a financial legacy requires a multifaceted approach that encompasses financial planning, investment strategies, risk management, estate planning, and more. It is not just about generating wealth. For people and families wishing to create a lasting financial legacy, this article seeks to offer insights and helpful guidance.

The significance of goal-setting

For the purpose of maintaining and expanding a financial legacy, it is crucial to set clear and defined financial goals. Goals act as a road map, directing people in the direction of their preferred financial outcomes.

This section discusses the value of setting goals and offers techniques for coming up with concrete, doable objectives.

Effective Money Management:

Wealth preservation and growth are based on effective financial planning. A person's current financial status must be evaluated, financial goals must be made, a budget and savings plan must be created, debt must be managed, an emergency fund must be established, and insurance must be obtained. Each of these topics is covered in detail in this part, along with helpful advice and methods for efficient money management.

Growth-Oriented Investment Strategies:

Growing a financial legacy requires careful investing. Key investment techniques like asset allocation, diversification, choosing the right investment vehicles, and knowing the difference between long-term and short-term investments are covered in this section. It also underlines how crucial it is to keep up with industry developments and adjust to shifting market dynamics.

Risk Administration

For the purpose of maintaining wealth and safeguarding a financial legacy, effective risk management is essential. This section goes through several areas of risk management, such as recognizing risk, figuring out your risk tolerance and appetite, putting hedging methods into practice, and using insurance to lessen your exposure to risk.

Estate Management:

Making a well-organized plan for the distribution of assets and money is a component of estate planning. This section examines the significance of estate planning and covers the components of a thorough estate plan, including the drafting of a will, the establishment of trusts, the handling of estate taxes, and updating beneficiary designations.

Education and communication left behind:

For the purpose of maintaining and expanding a financial legacy over generations, it is crucial to pass on financial values and expertise. This section emphasizes the value of encouraging open communication, teaching family members financial literacy, and supporting charitable initiatives as a way to leave a lasting legacy.

Accepting Technological Developments

Technology developments have completely changed the financial world, presenting both new opportunities and problems. The influence of financial technology (fintech), the function of algorithmic trading and robo-advisors, and the significance of online security and privacy are all covered in this section.

Managing Market and Economic Challenges:

The world economy is susceptible to changes and uncertainty. This section offers methods for overcoming economic and market difficulties, such as adjusting to market volatility, keeping a long-term perspective, and getting expert advice as necessary.

A comprehensive strategy including goal-setting, efficient financial planning, strategic investments, risk management, and estate planning is needed to preserve and expand a financial legacy. People can protect their money and leave a lasting financial legacy for future generations by employing these tactics and responding to changing conditions.

A variety of tactics and factors must be taken into account while preserving and expanding a financial legacy. It is essential to take proactive steps that protect wealth and encourage its expansion over time in a setting where the economy is always shifting. This in-depth article explores the various aspects of preserving and building a financial legacy, offering insights and helpful guidance for people and families looking to enjoy wealth and stability over the long term.

The importance of goal-setting is emphasized in the opening of the article. To lay out a plan for achieving one's intended financial outcomes, one must first establish clear and defined financial goals. Individuals can coordinate their financial decisions and behaviors by defining and prioritizing their objectives. The article examines several goal types, from short-term to long-term, and offers tips for creating realistic and reachable goals.

Wealth preservation and growth are based on effective financial planning. Starting with an evaluation of one's present financial condition, this part explores the various elements of financial planning. Individuals can obtain insight into their financial situation and pinpoint areas for development by analyzing their assets, obligations, income, and expenses. The essay then goes into detail about creating a budget, saving money, managing debt, and the value of having an emergency fund and having the right insurance coverage.

Another essential component of building a financial legacy is judicious investing. The article explores investment tactics like asset allocation, diversification, and picking the right investment vehicle that can help with long-term growth. In addition, it examines the distinction between long-term and short-term investments and emphasizes the significance of maintaining knowledge and flexibility in the face of shifting market conditions.

For the purpose of maintaining wealth and safeguarding a financial legacy, effective risk management is essential. This section goes through several areas of risk management, such as recognizing risk, figuring out your risk tolerance and appetite, putting hedging methods into practice, and using insurance to lessen your exposure to risk. People can safeguard their financial assets and guarantee the viability of their legacy by efficiently identifying and managing risks.

Estate planning is essential for maintaining and passing money down through the generations. The essay emphasizes the significance of estate planning and investigates the components of a thorough plan, including making a will, setting up trusts, preparing for estate taxes, and making sure beneficiary designations are current. People can make sure that their assets are dispersed in accordance with their preferences and reduce potential disputes among beneficiaries by being proactive with estate planning issues.

For a financial legacy to be maintained and expanded after a person's lifetime, it must be passed on along with financial values and knowledge. The essay emphasizes the significance of legacy education and communication, outlining methods for encouraging open discussion about finances, training family members financial literacy, and supporting charitable initiatives as a way to leave a lasting legacy.

The article also examines how technological developments affect leaving a financial legacy and growing it. It explores the function of financial technology (fintech), the advantages and drawbacks of using algorithmic trading and robo-advisors, and the significance of online security and privacy in protecting financial assets.

In order to protect and advance their financial legacies, people must negotiate the market and economy's obstacles. The global economy is prone to changes and uncertainty. A comprehensive strategy that includes goal-setting, efficient financial planning, strategic investments, risk management, estate planning, legacy education and communication, embracing technological advancements, and navigating economic and market challenges is needed to preserve and grow a financial legacy. The article offers strategies for adjusting to market volatility, maintaining a long-term perspective, and seeking professional guidance when necessary. Individuals can pave the road for a healthy financial future and leave a lasting legacy for future generations by comprehending and putting these fundamental ideas into practice.

Accepting Technological Developments

Technology improvements in the modern digital era have changed the financial environment, bringing both opportunities and challenges for maintaining and expanding a financial legacy. This section examines how financial technology (fintech) has affected wealth management and covers the advantages and drawbacks of using algorithmic trading and robo-advisors. Personalized solutions, faster procedures, and increased convenience are just a few of the ways that fintech has altered how people access and manage their financial assets. With the use of advanced algorithms, robo-advisors offer automated portfolio management and investment guidance to people with varied levels of financial education and expertise. With the use of market data and patterns, computer algorithms are used in algorithmic trading to quickly execute transactions with the potential for better returns. When using online financial platforms and services, it is crucial to be alert to issues with digital security and privacy.

The integrity of a financial legacy can be preserved by putting in place strong security measures and keeping up with the most recent cybersecurity techniques.

Managing Market and Economic Challenges:

The erratic and unstable nature of the world economy can make building and maintaining a financial legacy difficult. This section offers tactics for successfully overcoming market and economic difficulties to guarantee long-term financial stability. It's essential to adjust to market volatility since brief swings shouldn't overshadow a carefully thought-out investing strategy. The secret to surviving brief market downturns and seizing possible growth opportunities is to keep an eye on the long term. To navigate complex economic environments, it might be helpful to seek the advice of financial advisors and wealth managers who can offer insightful knowledge and experience. They can help with the creation of individualized strategies, portfolio rebalancing, and making defensible choices based on thorough market analysis. People can navigate economic and market crises while protecting and developing their financial legacies by staying informed about economic trends, keeping a diversified investment portfolio, and making disciplined investment decisions.

A thorough strategy that includes goal-setting, efficient financial planning, strategic investments, risk management, estate planning, legacy education and communication, embracing technological advancements, and navigating economic and market challenges is necessary to preserve and grow a financial legacy. Individuals may proactively protect their wealth, adjust to changing circumstances, and leave a lasting financial legacy for future generations by comprehending and putting five fundamental principles into practice.

Explain the significance of estate planning and the measures Dad took to guarantee a seamless transfer of wealth in paragraph 3.1.

A key component of wealth preservation and transfer is estate planning, which guarantees a seamless transfer of assets and reduces the likelihood of beneficiary disputes. It entails putting up a thorough plan that takes into account asset distribution, financial management, and the preservation of one's legacy after death. In the context of this paragraph, we'll talk about the value of estate planning and the measures Dad took to make sure the transfer of his fortune went well.

For people who want to keep ownership of their possessions and guarantee that their desires are carried out after death, estate planning is crucial. Without a suitable estate plan in place, the division of assets may be complicated legally and might give rise to family conflicts. People can create a framework that offers clarity, preserves their wealth, and brings peace of mind by proactively engaging in estate planning.

Dad understood the need of estate planning and made initiative to make sure that wealth was transferred smoothly. The writing of a will was one of his first actions. A will is a formal document that specifies how property will be distributed once someone passes away. Dad carefully drafted a will that specified how his assets should be distributed to his beneficiaries with the help of an estate planning lawyer. Dad made sure his intentions would be honored by having a will in place, reducing the possibility of potential family conflicts.

Dad also made a will and set up a number of trusts to better protect and manage his riches. Trusts offer flexibility and control over how assets are distributed, enabling precise directives to be fulfilled. Dad created a revocable living trust that allowed him to control his assets while he was alive and specify how they should be dispersed after his passing. Dad made sure that the transfer of assets went more smoothly by using trusts, possibly avoiding the probate procedure and all of its costs and delays.

Dad also carefully planned his estate taxes as a supplement to his estate plan. He was aware that the worth of his possessions and the fortune he hoped to leave to his beneficiaries could be greatly impacted by estate taxes. Dad sought advice from tax experts and put procedures into place, including donating assets while still alive, leveraging tax-exempt thresholds, and using techniques to reduce estate tax responsibilities. Dad made a conscious effort to arrange for estate taxes in order to increase the value of his estate and lessen the financial burden on his heirs and beneficiaries.

Dad understood the significance of reviewing and updating his estate plan on a regular basis to account for any changes in his financial situation or interpersonal ties. He was aware that certain life occurrences, such as marriage, divorce, childbirth, or death, could affect how assets were divided. He therefore made it a point to periodically review his estate plan and make any required modifications. Dad made sure that his preferences would be appropriately expressed and that his money would be allocated in accordance with his current intentions by being proactive and maintaining an up-to-date estate plan.

Dad also made open and honest communication with his family members about his estate plan a priority. He recognized the importance of clear communication in preventing potential misunderstandings and disputes among beneficiaries. Dad held family gatherings where he talked about his will, stated his goals, and answered any queries or concerns that his loved ones had. Estate planning is crucial to ensuring a smooth transfer of wealth and protecting one's legacy because it promotes transparency, reduces the likelihood of disputes, and ensures that his beneficiaries understand his wishes and the obligations associated with their inheritance. Dad understood this and proactively created a thorough estate plan.

He created trusts, prepared a will, planned for estate taxes, frequently updated his strategy, and encouraged open communication among his family members. By completing these steps, Dad avoided potential disputes among beneficiaries, made sure his assets were distributed in the manner he had intended, and left a lasting legacy for future generations.

3.2 Family business continuity: Discover how Dad prepared the following generation to carry on his entrepreneurial pursuits.

THE FINANCIAL LEGACY

A family business's long-term profitability and viability depend heavily on continuity. For many business owners, transferring their company to the next generation is important for both financial security and the preservation of their history and the principles that guide their entrepreneurial pursuits. Dad intentionally took action to prepare children for leadership roles because he saw the value of grooming the next generation to carry on his business. This article examines the methods and procedures Dad used to guarantee a smooth change in the company's leadership and promote a continuity-oriented culture.

Dad understood that setting an example for the next generation was the greatest way to raise them. He showed a commitment to the job, a great work ethic, and a love of the industry. The following generation was motivated to continue the family legacy by witnessing their father's dedication and excitement.

Early Business Exposure: Dad got the following generation started in the business at a young age. He would accompany them to the workplace, walk them through the procedures, and go over the problems and choices faced every day. This early exposure not only piqued their curiosity in the industry but also helped them comprehend its nuances better.

Education and Professional Development: Dad valued education and urged the younger generation to obtain advanced degrees and get essential credentials. Whether they connected to the main line of business or to other areas that could advance the company's success as a whole, he supported their interests and goals.

Mentoring and Advice: Dad served as a mentor to the younger generation, offering them suggestions and counsel throughout their professional lives. He made himself available for one-on-one conversations where he would impart his wisdom and experiences to assist people in overcoming obstacles and coming to wise judgments.

rotating responsibilities and Skill Development: Dad established a rotating program where the following generation would spend time in various departments and responsibilities inside the company in order to prepare them for leadership. They were able to get a comprehensive understanding of the business's operations as well as a broad range of talents thanks to this.

Dad urged the following generation to think creatively and to take into account new business chances. He would push them to think beyond the box and encouraged them to research and experiment with new concepts.

Building a solid Leadership Team: Dad was aware that a solid leadership team was just as important to the future of the family business as the next generation. In order to fill leadership positions, he sought for and developed bright executives from both inside and beyond the family. Dad made sure the family business would be prepared to meet difficulties and grab development opportunities by developing a diversified and talented leadership team.

Participation in Decision-Making: Dad valued the contribution of the younger generation to the decision-making process. He would get their opinions on significant business issues and include them in discussions that were crucial. They felt empowered and had a sense of ownership in the company as a result of their involvement.

Promoting an Accountability Culture: Dad helped create an atmosphere of responsibility and accountability within the family business. He instilled a sense of pride and a dedication to the success of the company in the next generation by encouraging them to take responsibility for their actions and choices.

Developing Interpersonal and Communication Skills: Dad emphasized the value of developing interpersonal and communication skills in order to prepare the next generation for leadership positions. He urged them to actively listen, communicate their views clearly, and cultivate strong bonds with coworkers, clients, and other employees.

Encouragement of Lifelong Learning: Dad worked to instill a culture of lifelong learning and growth within the family business. In order to keep up with the most recent developments and industry best practices, he advised the younger generation to attend workshops, seminars, and professional conferences. They were able to keep ahead of the curve and adjust to a corporate climate that was changing quickly because to this emphasis on continual learning.

Dad was aware of the importance of solid succession planning for the survival of the family business. He collaborated closely with experts to create a thorough succession plan that described how to hand over control and ownership to the following generation. Individual capabilities, interests, and the company's general vision were all taken into account in this plan. Dad engaged the following generation in succession planning, making sure that their dreams and objectives were incorporated into the strategy.

Building a Solid corporate Culture: Dad understood the value of building a solid corporate culture in promoting continuity and unity within the organization. Core values like honesty, cooperation, and customer focus that he established were the standards for the following generation. Their actions and choices were more in line with the family business's overarching vision and mission thanks to this common culture.

Dad managed to strike a balance between giving the next generation autonomy and providing direction when it was required. He gave them the freedom to make choices and take chances, which enabled them to grow as leaders and learn from their mistakes. At the same time, he was always there to offer assistance and direction whenever they needed it or had questions.

Dad was a firm believer in the ability of family gatherings to foster harmony and continuity within the family company. He set up frequent gatherings for the family to discuss business, give updates, and coordinate goals and plans. These gatherings also served as a forum for open discussion, enabling family members to resolve any issues or problems amicably.

Dad was able to successfully prepare the next generation to carry on his entrepreneurial activities by using these techniques and ideas. Because of the continuity he created, the family firm was certain to prosper for many generations while upholding its essential principles and experiencing sustainable growth. The following generation was well-equipped to lead the company into the future, preserving the family legacy and ensuring its ongoing prosperity thanks to the knowledge, abilities, and values instilled by their father.

Collaboration and Teamwork Encouraged: Dad promoted a collaborative and cooperative attitude throughout the family business. He urged the younger generation to collaborate and take advantage of one another's talents. They developed the effective collaboration and solid working connections necessary for future leadership roles through cross-functional teams and collaborative initiatives.

Dad understood the value of exposing the next generation to viewpoints and experiences from outside the family. He urged them to attend trade shows, social gatherings, and organizations for professionals. They widened their horizons, brought new ideas back to the family firm, and connected with industry experts and other business environments.

Emphasizing Ethical Business Practices: Dad recognized the value of ethical business practices in upholding the credibility and reputation of the family firm. Instilling in the next generation a strong sense of ethics and integrity, he emphasized the value of conducting business with honesty, transparency, and fairness. He made sure that the family firm would prosper in the long run by emphasizing moral conduct.

Creating Opportunities for Leadership Development: Dad went out of his way to find chances for the younger generation to grow as leaders. He urged students to assume leadership positions in neighborhood associations, humanitarian projects, and professional organizations. Through these encounters, they were able to develop their leadership skills, expand their networks, and support causes outside of the family business.

Adopting Innovation and Technology: Dad understood the revolutionary potential of technology and the need for ongoing innovation. He urged the younger generation to keep up with technical developments and look into how to use technology to expand businesses.

Dad made sure the family business remained competitive and ready to respond to changing trends and customer expectations by creating an innovative culture.

Promoting Risk-Taking: Dad was aware that becoming an entrepreneur required taking measured risks. He exhorted the younger generation to take calculated risks within a set of rules. He encouraged the next generation to be resilient and innovative by giving them the flexibility to experiment with new ideas and by helping them through the ups and downs of business operations.

Dad understood the need of financial literacy in managing a successful business, and he actively promotes it. He made certain that the following generation received thorough instruction and training in financial management, including comprehension of financial statements, planning for the future financially, and budgeting. They were able to make wise judgments because to their financial savvy, which also helped the family business grow sustainably.

Dad instilled in the next generation the value of a customer-centric perspective by helping them to develop one. He underlined the need of getting to know clients well and being aware of their wants and preferences. The following generation learnt to prioritize customer happiness, loyalty, and retention—a crucial factor in long-term corporate success —by concentrating on providing excellent customer experiences.

The ability to adjust to shifting market circumstances is something that Dad taught the following generation. He urged them to be abreast of business developments, technology advances, and shifting consumer tastes. They might find new opportunities and guide the family firm toward continuous success by staying adaptable and receptive to changes in the business environment.

Maintaining the Family Legacy: Dad emphasized the importance of maintaining the family legacy above all else. He told tales about the family's entrepreneurial journey, the difficulties they encountered, and the principles that guided their success. He made sure that the following generation would carry on the family tradition with respect and a strong sense of duty by instilling a sense of pride in the family heritage.

Dad made extensive, varied efforts to develop the next generation and maintain the family company. Dad helped the next generation succeed in continuing his entrepreneurial endeavors by setting an example, providing education and professional development, encouraging mentorship and guidance, fostering a culture of innovation and collaboration, and emphasizing values like integrity and customer-centricity. The family firm was positioned for continued success while upholding the history and principles Dad had established thanks to their combined knowledge, abilities, and shared vision.

3.3 Philanthropic activities: Focus on Dad's philanthropic works and the lessons he taught the author about contributing to society.

A full and socially responsible existence must include philanthropy and giving back to the community. Dad was aware of the significance of utilizing his wealth and resources to improve the world. He had faith in the ability of charity to deal with societal problems, advance worthwhile causes, and leave a long-lasting legacy of kindness and giving. The author's principles of giving back to society and Dad's charity donations will be highlighted in this essay.

Early Influence and ideals: Dad's dedication to philanthropy was a result of the ideals he was taught from a young age and his upbringing. He was raised in a household that valued kindness, empathy, and civic responsibility. These principles laid the groundwork for his charitable undertakings and influenced his view of the transformative potential of charitable giving.

Dad approached charitable giving with a strategic perspective. He carefully chose organizations and causes that shared his principles and made a substantial contribution to society. He made sure that his philanthropic efforts were focused on programs and activities that would make a real and lasting influence by conducting in-depth study and working with experts in the field.

THE FINANCIAL LEGACY

Dad made large financial contributions to a number of causes as part of his philanthropic activities. He recognized the importance of financial resources in enabling organizations to successfully carry out their purposes. His kind contributions helped address important societal concerns including poverty, injustice, and environmental preservation by providing funding for research, supporting educational programs, offering healthcare services, and so on.

Collaboration and Partnerships: Dad understood that working together was essential to enhancing the impact of his generosity. To take advantage of group resources and experience, he formed alliances with like-minded people, businesses, and nonprofits. These partnerships made it possible to solve societal problems with better efficiency, efficacy, and reach.

Engagement and Volunteering: Dad valued active involvement in philanthropy above and beyond monetary donations. He exhorted the writers and their relatives to donate their time and talents to help worthy organizations. They experienced firsthand the importance of hands-on involvement and a personal dedication to making a difference, whether they were taking part in community service initiatives, planning fundraising activities, or providing pro bono services.

Dad's charitable efforts extended beyond offering temporary comfort, instead focusing on developing long-term solutions. He supported the development of long-lasting answers to systemic problems. He backed programs that emphasized developing community capacity, empowering underprivileged groups, and tackling the underlying causes of social issues. Dad hoped to bring about long-lasting beneficial change by funding sustainable development initiatives.

Dad saw the potential of social entrepreneurship to spur innovation and produce long-lasting social impact. He promoted an ecosystem of entrepreneurial initiatives that addressed urgent social and environmental problems by supporting social entrepreneurs that combined business savvy with a humanitarian commitment. Dad promoted creative solutions that would ultimately benefit society by encouraging social entrepreneurs.

Dad was a strong believer in the transforming potential of education. He thought that in order for people to realize their greatest potential, they needed to have access to high-quality education. In order to help poor students pursue higher education and provide them the tools to improve their lives and the lives of their communities, he financed educational institutions and scholarships.

Dad was aware of the significance of environmental conservation and the need to safeguard the earth for upcoming generations. He backed groups that worked to protect natural habitats, advance sustainable lifestyles, and spread knowledge about climate change. He wanted to help make the world a healthier and more sustainable place through his charitable work.

Motivating Others: Dad's philanthropy extended beyond monetary donations. He wanted to encourage others to support the cause and change the world. He aimed to inspire others to take on social responsibility and to use their skills and resources to address societal problems by sharing his philanthropic path and the effects of his donations.

The author was raised with strong, enduring ideals that included giving back to society. The author learnt the value of empathy, compassion, and social responsibility while growing up in a home where charity played a significant role in their family's identity. Dad's charitable actions served as an example and motivated the author to carry on the tradition of altruism in the family.

The author recognized that philanthropy involved more than just monetary donations; it also involved active participation, volunteer work, and strategic planning. They discovered how to choose causes and groups that shared their values and how to deploy their resources wisely for the greatest possible impact.

In addition, the author carried on Dad's commitment to finding long-lasting answers and tackling the underlying causes of social problems. They understood how interrelated social, economic, and environmental problems were and worked to promote programs that sought comprehensive, long-term solutions.

A great sense of gratitude for their own blessings and a profound knowledge of their ability to have a positive impact on others were instilled in the author by their father's charity. Like their father, they accepted the obligation to use their power, abilities, and riches for the benefit of society.

Dad left a long legacy of kindness, generosity, and social effect because of his charitable work and the principles he established in the author about giving back to society. Dad's charity not only met immediate needs but also established the groundwork for a more equal, just, and sustainable future through strategic giving, active involvement, collaborations, and a dedication to sustainable solutions. By launching their own charitable efforts and being inspired by the ideals and life lessons their father taught them, the author continues to uphold their father's legacy.

A full and socially responsible existence must include philanthropy and giving back to the community. Dad was aware of the significance of utilizing his wealth and resources to improve the world.

He had faith in the ability of charity to deal with societal problems, advance worthwhile causes, and leave a long-lasting legacy of kindness and giving. The author's principles of giving back to society and Dad's charity donations will be highlighted in this essay.

Early Influence and ideals: Dad's dedication to philanthropy was a result of the ideals he was taught from a young age and his upbringing. He was raised in a household that valued kindness, empathy, and civic responsibility. These principles laid the groundwork for his charitable undertakings and influenced his view of the transformative potential of charitable giving.

Dad approached charitable giving with a strategic perspective. He carefully chose organizations and causes that shared his principles and made a substantial contribution to society. He made sure that his philanthropic efforts were focused on programs and activities that would make a real and lasting influence by conducting in-depth study and working with experts in the field.

Dad made large financial contributions to a number of causes as part of his philanthropic activities. He recognized the importance of financial resources in enabling organizations to successfully carry out their purposes. His kind contributions helped address important societal concerns including poverty, injustice, and environmental preservation by providing funding for research, supporting educational programs, offering healthcare services, and so on.

Collaboration and Partnerships: Dad understood that working together was essential to enhancing the impact of his generosity. To take advantage of group resources and experience, he formed alliances with like-minded people, businesses, and nonprofits. These partnerships made it possible to solve societal problems with better efficiency, efficacy, and reach.

Engagement and Volunteering: Dad valued active involvement in philanthropy above and beyond monetary donations. He exhorted the writers and their relatives to donate their time and talents to help worthy organizations. They experienced firsthand the importance of hands-on involvement and a personal dedication to making a difference, whether they were taking part in community service initiatives, planning fundraising activities, or providing pro bono services.

Dad's charitable efforts extended beyond offering temporary comfort, instead focusing on developing long-term solutions. He supported the development of long-lasting answers to systemic problems. He backed programs that emphasized developing community capacity, empowering underprivileged groups, and tackling the underlying causes of social issues. Dad hoped to bring about long-lasting beneficial change by funding sustainable development initiatives.

Dad saw the potential of social entrepreneurship to spur innovation and produce long-lasting social impact. He promoted an ecosystem of entrepreneurial initiatives that addressed urgent social and environmental problems by supporting social entrepreneurs that combined business savvy with a humanitarian commitment. Dad promoted creative solutions that would ultimately benefit society by encouraging social entrepreneurs.

Dad was a strong believer in the transforming potential of education. He thought that in order for people to realize their greatest potential, they needed to have access to high-quality education. In order to help poor students pursue higher education and provide them the tools to improve their lives and the lives of their communities, he financed educational institutions and scholarships.

Dad was aware of the significance of environmental conservation and the need to safeguard the earth for upcoming generations. He backed groups that worked to protect natural habitats, advance sustainable lifestyles, and spread knowledge about climate change. He wanted to help make the world a healthier and more sustainable place through his charitable work.

Motivating Others: Dad's philanthropy extended beyond monetary donations. He wanted to encourage others to support the cause and change the world. He aimed to inspire others to take on social responsibility and to use their skills and resources to address societal problems by sharing his philanthropic path and the effects of his donations.

The author was raised with strong, enduring ideals that included giving back to society. The author learnt the value of empathy, compassion, and social responsibility while growing up in a home where charity played a significant role in their family's identity. Dad's charitable actions served as an example and motivated the author to carry on the tradition of altruism in the family.

The author recognized that philanthropy involved more than just monetary donations; it also involved active participation, volunteer work, and strategic planning. They discovered how to choose causes and groups that shared their values and how to deploy their resources wisely for the greatest possible impact.

In addition, the author carried on Dad's commitment to finding long-lasting answers and tackling the underlying causes of social problems. They understood how interrelated social, economic, and environmental problems were and worked to promote programs that sought comprehensive, long-term solutions.

A great sense of gratitude for their own blessings and a profound knowledge of their ability to have a positive impact on others were instilled in the author by their father's charity. Like their father, they accepted the obligation to use their power, abilities, and riches for the benefit of society.

Dad left a long legacy of kindness, generosity, and social effect because of his charitable work and the principles he established in the author about giving back to society. Dad's charity not only met immediate needs but also established the groundwork for a more equal, just, and sustainable future through strategic giving, active involvement, collaborations, and a dedication to sustainable solutions. By launching their own charitable efforts and being inspired by the ideals and life lessons their father taught them, the author continues to uphold their father's legacy.

Chapter 4

Chapter 4:
Lessons for Future Generations

Each generation passes on a plethora of information, experiences, and lessons learnt as it hands the torch to the following one. Future generations might use these lessons as a guide by learning about the successes, setbacks, and knowledge accumulated in the past. It is essential to summarize the most vital lessons for future generations in our rapidly changing environment. The purpose of this essay is to examine some important lessons that can act as a guide for individuals who will create the world of the future.

1: Accept Change and Be Adaptable

The environment we live in is always changing as a result of technological developments, cultural shifts, and international problems. Future generations must embrace change and foster adaptation as fundamental qualities. Success will depend on one's capacity to survive and thrive in situations that change quickly. Lessons learned in the past show that people who fought change frequently ended up being left behind. Future generations may seize opportunities, innovate, and cultivate resilience in the face of uncertainty by embracing change.

2: Maintain and safeguard the environment

The state of our environment is one of the biggest problems that humanity is now facing. Future generations must emphasize the preservation and protection of the natural world in order to avoid repeating the mistakes of the past. The repercussions of careless resource extraction, pollution, and disdain for the delicate balance of ecosystems are highlighted by lessons learned from the past. Future generations can contribute to the restoration and preservation of the environment for future generations by adopting sustainable activities, embracing renewable energy sources, and putting in place responsible regulations.

Promote international collaboration and understanding

The connectivity of our world has become more and more apparent, as global issues like climate change, pandemics, and economic interdependence demand unprecedented levels of cooperation. Future generations must recognize how crucial it is to promote international harmony and understanding. History's lessons highlight the necessity for communication, empathy, and common objectives by demonstrating the divisive power of conflicts and divisions. Future generations can contribute to a more peaceful and united world by embracing variety, fostering intercultural understanding, and encouraging peaceful resolutions.

4: Give education and lifelong learning top priority

The foundation of development and empowerment is education. Future generations must value education as a lifelong endeavour and understand its transforming power. Lessons from the past show how information has the power to reshape civilizations, spark innovation, and advance social mobility.

Future generations may arm themselves with the skills required to survive in a world that is always changing by making investments in strong educational systems, encouraging critical thinking, and cultivating a love of learning.

Adopt a diversity and inclusion mindset.

The world is a patchwork of various cultures, customs, and viewpoints. Future generations must comprehend the inherent worth of valuing inclusiveness and diversity. Lessons from history show the injustices and conflicts brought on by prejudice and exclusion while also illuminating the richness and power that result from inclusive communities. Future generations may build a more equitable and peaceful world that fully realizes the potential of each of its citizens by cultivating inclusivity, advancing equality, and honoring variety.

Practice compassion and empathy.

Future generations must understand the value of empathy and compassion in a time of rising individuality and technology breakthroughs that can distance us from one another. The transforming potential of empathy in creating understanding, mending wounds, and fostering social cohesiveness is demonstrated by lessons from the past. Future generations may cross barriers, create meaningful connections, and tackle today's most critical social and humanitarian issues by developing empathy, actively listening to others, and exhibiting compassion.

Take Advantage of Ethical Technological Advances

Every area of human life has been altered by technology progress, and many more technical advances will be made in the decades to come. However, there are ethical issues that must be taken into account in addition to the advantages. Future generations must ensure that

technical advancement is constrained by moral values by taking the lessons of the past to heart. Future generations may harness the potential of technology for the greater good while avoiding the traps of its exploitation by prioritizing privacy, responsibility, and the welfare of individuals and societies.

Future generations can learn valuable lessons from the accumulated knowledge and experiences of those who have come before them. Future generations may create a world that is more sustainable, inclusive, and just by accepting change, prioritizing environmental protection, developing international cooperation, promoting education, embracing diversity, engaging in acts of empathy, and morally embracing technical breakthroughs. Future leaders, innovators, and changemakers can use these lessons as a compass to help them navigate the intricacies of the world and strive toward building a better future for everybody. Future generations must take note of these lessons and work to create a society that upholds the principles of development, compassion, and harmony.

8: Promote emotional and mental health

Future generations must place a higher priority on their mental and emotional health at a time of information overload, continual connectivity, and mounting societal demands. The implications of disregarding mental health, such as the rise in anxiety, depression, and burnout rates, are highlighted through historical lessons. Future generations may promote resilience, balance, and general well-being in their personal and professional life by supporting self-care routines, encouraging candid conversation about mental health, and placing a high value on emotional intelligence.

Practice Responsible Production and Consumption (9).

Resources are being depleted, waste is being accumulated, and the environment is being harmed as a result of the current consumer-driven culture's unsustainable patterns of consumption and production. Responsible consumption and production must be taught to future generations. Lessons from the past emphasize how crucial it is to practice sustainable living, reduce waste, and consume with awareness. Future generations may help create a more sustainable and just society by making thoughtful decisions, encouraging systemic change, and buying from ethical and environmentally responsible companies.

10: Promote equality and social justice

In all civilizations, there is still a constant battle for social justice and equality. Future generations must comprehend the significance of upholding these ideals and making a concerted effort to create a society that is more equitable and egalitarian. History teaches us about the severe repercussions of systemic injustice, discrimination, and oppression. Future generations may break down barriers and build a society where everyone has equal chances and rights by questioning cultural conventions, fighting for equal rights, and elevating underrepresented voices.

11: Accept Failure and Gain Knowledge from Mistakes

Future generations must learn to accept failure as a necessary part of life and as a good learning opportunity. Lessons from history show that several failures and setbacks resulted in many great accomplishments and breakthroughs. Future generations can acquire a growth mindset and overcome challenges on their journey to individual and societal prosperity by reframing failure as a stepping stone to success, fostering resilience, and learning from mistakes.

Encourage moral leadership and governance (12)

To effectively address the complex issues that nations face, effective leadership and governance are crucial. The common good must be prioritized by future generations as they draw on the knowledge of the past. History provides examples of the effects of power abuse, authoritarianism, and corruption. Future generations can develop institutions that maintain justice and democracy by encouraging openness, accountability, and moral decision-making. This will help to build trust, foster social cohesion, and promote future generations.

13: Recognize the Power of Networking and Collaboration

Networking and collaboration are more important in today's linked environment. Future generations must understand the value of cross-generational cooperation and collaborative action. The transformative power of movements, alliances, and partnerships is shown by historical lessons. Future generations can increase their effect, resolve complicated issues, and affect good change on a global scale through developing relationships, creating networks, and cooperating toward common goals.

Keep Cultural Heritage Safe and Welcome Creativity

A monument to the rich tapestry of human history and identity is cultural heritage. Future generations must learn to embrace creativity and innovation while appreciating and preserving their cultural legacy. The value of cultural preservation, artistic expression, and the persuasiveness of narrative are emphasized by lessons from the past. Future generations can honor their heritage while pushing the limits of creativity and innovation by recognizing cultural variety, supporting the arts, and encouraging knowledge transfer between generations.

15: Leave Future Generations a Positive Legacy

In the end, younger generations must understand that it is up to them to leave a good legacy for those who come after. Lessons from the past highlight how the decisions and deeds of earlier generations have shaped the world we live in today. Future generations can create a better society than the one they inherited by acting with integrity, empathy, and a long-term perspective. This will have a good and long-lasting effect on future generations.

Future generations should learn a wide range of teachings that touch on all facets of personal, societal, and global existence. By promoting social fairness, responsible consumption, mental and emotional health, acceptance of failure, and mental and emotional well-being

Future generations may create a society that is more sustainable, equitable, and prosperous by practicing ethical leadership, encouraging collaboration, protecting cultural heritage, and leaving a positive legacy. These lessons act as a set of guiding principles that encourage upcoming innovators, changemakers, and leaders to pave the way for a better and more promising future. Future generations must take note of these teachings, meet the difficulties of their time head-on, and build a world that represents the principles of kindness, justice, and development.

16: Encourage media literacy and critical thinking

Future generations must develop media literacy and critical thinking abilities at a time of information overload and pervasive misinformation. The power of propaganda, fake news, and information manipulation is revealed by historical lessons. Future generations will be better able to make decisions, participate in constructive debate, and contribute to an educated and democratic society if they learn to assess, analyze, and critically think about the information that is offered to them.

17: Encourage entrepreneurship and innovation

Entrepreneurship and innovation are important forces behind society advancement and economic success. Future generations must embrace the spirit of entrepreneurship and creativity, utilizing cutting-edge technology and original ideas to solve critical problems. Historical examples show the transformative potential of ground-breaking discoveries and business endeavors. Future generations may build a robust and dynamic global economy by encouraging an innovation culture, rewarding risk-taking, and supporting entrepreneurial initiatives.

18: Encourage wellness and good health

Future generations should place a high premium on the health and well-being of people in both groups and as individuals. Lessons learned from the past highlight the significance of readily available healthcare, disease prevention, and mental wellness. Future generations may build a society where everyone has the chance to live a happy and healthy life by promoting healthy behaviors, making investments in healthcare systems, and placing a high priority on mental health assistance.

Practice moral and ethical AI development.

A number of facets of human life could be revolutionized by artificial intelligence (AI). Future generations must, however, approach the creation of AI with moral sensitivity and responsible behavior. Lessons from the past highlight the dangers of AI, including algorithmic biases and privacy violations. Future generations may guarantee that AI technologies are used for the benefit of humanity while avoiding possible harm by giving priority to ethical AI frameworks, transparency, and human-centered design.

Accept the Strength of Compassionate Leadership (20)

For society to be just and compassionate, compassionate leadership is necessary. Future generations must recognize the value of compassionate leadership, whereby leaders put their constituents' needs first, promote inclusivity, and stand up for underrepresented groups. The transforming power of caring leaders who have devoted their lives to promoting social justice and equality is demonstrated by lessons learned from history. Future generations may encourage positive change and build a society that values compassion and fairness by having people in positions of authority who exhibit empathy, integrity, and humility.

21: Encourage resiliency in the face of hardship

In order to be resilient in the face of difficulties, future generations must learn that adversity is an unavoidable part of life. Lessons from the past show how resilient people and communities can be when faced with adversity and tragedy. Future generations may bounce back from failures, overcome difficulties, and prosper in the face of adversity through cultivating resilience skills, cultivating mental and emotional strength, and creating supportive communities.

22: Encourage collaboration between generations

For a society to be sustainable and cohesive, cooperation between generations is essential. Future generations must encourage intergenerational cooperation, recognizing the expertise and knowledge of older generations while embracing the fresh ideas and viewpoints of the younger ones. Lessons from the past show the effectiveness of intergenerational communication and cooperation in promoting societal advancement.

Future generations can develop a society where all age groups contribute to a common future vision by building forums for meaningful discussion, mutual respect, and cooperation.

The lessons for future generations cover a wide range of topics, including innovation, compassion, and resilience as well as media literacy, critical thinking, and media literacy. Future generations will be better able to negotiate the difficulties and complexities of a constantly changing environment by embracing critical thinking, engaging in ethical AI development, encouraging intergenerational collaboration, and fostering ethical leadership. Future generations can create a society that is marked by growth, empathy, sustainability, and inclusivity by adopting these lessons. Future generations may create a society that is more affluent, just, and peaceful for everyone by incorporating these teachings into their individual and collective journeys.

4.1 Fostering financial literacy: Highlight the significance of educating kids about money.

The significance of teaching children financial literacy cannot be emphasized in a society that is becoming more complex and financially driven. Our lives are heavily influenced by money, which affects our opportunities, decisions, and general well-being. Giving kids the fundamental knowledge and abilities in money management, saving, investing, and budgeting will enable them to make wise financial decisions, develop sound financial practices, and confidently navigate the financial world. This essay examines the value of introducing children to the concept of money while emphasizing the advantages of early financial education.

Knowledge of the Value of Money

Financial literacy is fundamentally about knowing the worth of money and how it functions in society. Early money education fosters in young children an understanding of the time and work required to earn money. Children can start to understand the relationship between work, money, and the resources it provides by discussing ideas like earning an income, the importance of saving, and the effects of spending. This knowledge serves as the cornerstone for prudent money management and a lifelong awareness of the worth of money.

laying solid financial groundwork

Early financial literacy instruction lays a solid basis for future financial success. Children who study money management acquire critical abilities including budgeting, saving, and separating wants from requirements. They can build sound spending habits and careful financial decisions thanks to these abilities. By

We give kids the skills they need for long-term financial security and stability by teaching them the value of setting financial goals, keeping track of costs, and making wise decisions.

fostering consumer awareness and responsible spending

It is crucial to teach kids about responsible spending and consumer awareness in today's consumer-driven world. Children who receive financial literacy instruction are better able to grasp the repercussions of impulsive purchases, the effects of debt, and the significance of differentiating between needs and wants. Children learn to prioritize their finances, make careful spending decisions, and stay out of debt by being taught the concept of delayed gratification.

Children who are taught about consumer rights and duties grow up to be discerning shoppers who make wise financial decisions and avoid falling into scams.

Promoting Long-Term Financial Planning and Savings:

Savings are the cornerstone of future wealth building and financial stability. Children who learn the practice of saving early on develop a long-term financial planning perspective. Children can create a financial cushion and achieve their objectives when we teach them about the value of compounding, the advantages of setting away a percentage of their money, and the significance of saving for emergencies and the future. Children who learn to save and make plans for the future develop a sense of financial independence and resilience that equips them to face obstacles and seize opportunities.

Introducing the Basic Investment Concepts:

Even though it may seem complicated, teaching kids the fundamentals of investing paves the way for a lifetime of wise financial choices. By explaining to kids the potential rewards, risks, and advantages of investing, this area of personal finance is made less mysterious. Children can better grasp how their money might increase in value over time by being taught ideas like diversification, compound interest, and the significance of a long-term investing horizon. Children can learn the value of investing and form a favorable outlook on long-term wealth growth by getting started young.

Creating a Financial Independence and Entrepreneurial Mindset:

Education in financial literacy also promotes financial independence and an entrepreneurial perspective. By educating kids on entrepreneurship, the importance of creativity and invention, as well as the benefits and difficulties of establishing a firm, we provide them the tools they need to think creatively and cultivate an entrepreneurial spirit. Children who are financially literate are aware of the value of diversifying their sources of income, looking for opportunities, and taking calculated risks. Children are put on the route to financial independence with the help of this mindset, which fosters self-reliance, adaptability, and a proactive approach to financial decision-making.

Promoting Responsible Borrowing and Debt Management

Children will probably come across circumstances where borrowing and managing debt become required as they become older and enter adults. Their knowledge and abilities are improved through financial literacy instruction, enabling them to handle these circumstances properly. We equip kids to make wise borrowing decisions by educating them about credit, interest rates, available borrowing options, and the negative effects of having too much debt. This information enables people to steer clear of debt pitfalls and responsibly handle their financial commitments, protecting their financial security.

Getting Kids Ready for Financial Reality:

Children who are taught about money are better prepared for the adult financial challenges they will encounter. It aids in their comprehension of issues like income, taxes, spending budgeting, and the significance of retirement financial planning.

By giving kids this information, we give them the power to take charge of their financial lives, make wise financial decisions, and confidently negotiate the complexity of personal finance. With the knowledge and tools needed to create a stable and prosperous future, children may transition into adulthood with confidence.

Instilling financial literacy in youngsters is crucial in a time when financial systems are becoming more complex and economies are becoming more consumer-driven. We give children the skills and knowledge needed to successfully navigate the financial landscape by teaching them about the value of money, laying strong financial foundations, encouraging responsible spending and saving habits, introducing concepts of investing, cultivating an entrepreneurial mindset, and preparing them for financial realities. Children who get early financial education are better equipped to make wise choices, develop sound financial practices, and assure a bright future. By educating our kids about money, we ensure their long-term financial security and give them the power to control their own financial futures.

Teaching kids about money management and financial literacy is more crucial than ever in the complex and financially driven world of today. Children who are financially literate are better equipped to negotiate the intricacies of the financial world, make wise financial decisions, and develop sound financial habits. One of your most important duties as a father is to instill financial literacy in your kids. In order to inculcate financial literacy in their children, dads can use the ideas shared in this post, which also emphasizes the significance of teaching kids about money management.

The Value of Teaching Children Money Management Skills:

For children's future financial stability, it is crucial to teach them about money management. Understanding how to efficiently handle money is essential for both personal and financial success since it permeates all part of our life. We can equip kids with the knowledge and skills they need to make wise financial decisions by teaching them about money management. Additionally, educating kids about money management fosters a sense of independence, resiliency, and self-confidence, giving them lifelong abilities.

Dad's Financial Literacy Teaching Techniques:

Set a good example:

Dads may teach their children about money management most effectively by setting a good example. Children see their parents' financial habits and pick them up. Dads may be a good financial role model for their kids by practicing appropriate money management techniques including budgeting, saving, and investing. Sharing personal financial experiences, talking about financial choices, and including kids in family financial talks can all help kids grasp how money management principles are used in the real world.

Make it enjoyable and begin early:

Early financial literacy instruction for children is essential. Dad might begin by engaging kids in age-appropriate activities and games that introduce them to fundamental financial ideas. Children can learn about the worth of money, budgeting, and making decisions, for instance, by setting up a pretend store or by being given a little allowance.

Making Financial education that is fun and engaging for kids builds a strong foundation for future financial learning and encourages them to manage their money well.

Teach Children to Value Saving:

A key component of effective money management is saving. Dad may instill a habit of saving by assisting kids in creating savings objectives, such as saving for a gift or a special outing. gifting kids clear containers to separate their money into spending, saving, and gifting categories might help them understand the value of saving visually. Dad might also teach his children about interest by offering to match a portion of their savings. This method instills a sense of long-term financial planning in children and encourages them to form disciplined saving habits.

Children Should Be Involved in Financial Decision-Making:

Children who are involved in age-appropriate financial decision-making processes are better able to comprehend the effects of their decisions. Dad can involve the kids in creating the family budget, comparing prices while shopping, and choosing family outings or vacation destinations within a predetermined budget. Children that are involved in this process learn how to think critically, evaluate trade-offs, and make thoughtful purchasing decisions. Additionally, it fosters a sense of accountability and responsibility for financial decisions.

How to Distinguish Between Needs and Wants

An essential part of financial literacy is knowing the difference between requirements and wants. Dad can assist kids in making the distinction between discretionary wants like gadgets or entertainment and basic requirements like food, shelter, and education. Having discussions about priorities, establishing boundaries, and

Making informed choices based on needs and wants promotes appropriate spending behaviors and aids in the development of financial discipline in youngsters.

Describe the Foundations of Investing:

Even though it might seem complicated, dads can teach their kids the fundamentals of investing. Children can better comprehend the advantages of investing their money if the topics of long-term growth, compound interest, and the need of early investing are discussed. Dad can describe straightforward investing possibilities like savings accounts or low-risk investment options, and you can follow the development together. The foundation for future financial progress and a proactive approach to wealth creation are laid by this early exposure to investment.

Promote entrepreneurial thought:

Dads can help their kids develop an entrepreneurial mindset by fostering their capacity for creativity, invention, and problem-solving. This way of thinking fosters a sense of independence in terms of finances, adaptability, and self-reliance. Dad can talk to his kids about entrepreneurship, tell them success stories, and inspire them to consider their own business ideas.

With the aid of this strategy, kids can learn about numerous sources of revenue, how to generate income, and the importance of entrepreneurship as a means of achieving financial success.

Dads have a crucial role to play in educating kids about financial literacy and money management. Dads give their kids the knowledge, abilities, and mindset required for both personal and financial success by establishing financial literacy in them. Dads can empower their children by setting an example, starting early, making financial education fun, teaching the value of saving, including kids in financial decision-making, separating necessities from wants, introducing the fundamentals of investment, and promoting entrepreneurial thinking.

to teach kids how to negotiate the intricacies of the financial world, make informed financial decisions, and develop healthy financial habits. Dads give their kids a strong foundation for a happy and secure future by instilling financial literacy in them.

4.2 Fostering the entrepreneurial spirit: Learn how the author's perspective was influenced by Dad's support of entrepreneurship.

A strong force behind invention, economic expansion, and personal joy is the entrepreneurial spirit. The development of this spirit in people, especially in their formative years, can have a significant impact on their outlook and future endeavors. In this essay, the author examines the value of fostering the entrepreneurial spirit and how the author's father's support of it influenced her outlook.

We hope to raise awareness of the transforming impact of promoting entrepreneurship and its long-lasting consequences on a person's viewpoint and goals by sharing personal experiences and ideas.

Fostering the Entrepreneurial Spirit: Its Importance

In today's environment of rapid change, encouraging the entrepreneurial spirit is essential. Entrepreneurship embodies qualities like innovation, adaptability, risk-taking, and problem-solving that are crucial for individual development, economic prosperity, and society advancement. People who are encouraged to be entrepreneurial have the knowledge and outlook needed to spot opportunities, solve problems, and come up with novel solutions. Additionally, entrepreneurship cultivates a sense of independence, adaptability, and a proactive outlook on life, enabling people to control their own fate and have a significant impact on the world.

Father's Support for Entrepreneurship

The author's father was crucial in fostering her entrepreneurial mentality. He saw the advantages of encouraging a worldview that emphasized creativity, independence, and pursuing one's hobbies. Dad always encouraged the author to pursue their passions, take calculated chances, and enjoy the difficulties that come with being an entrepreneur. The author felt empowered to dream large, think outside the box, and seize possibilities for growth and self-discovery because of his support and direction in that atmosphere.

Making a Friendly Environment

Dad fostered an environment that was encouraging to anyone with an entrepreneurial spirit. He encouraged free dialogue, the value of ideas, and the appreciation of creativity. Dad provided a safe environment for ideation and the exploration of entrepreneurial ideas, encouraging the author to voice their thoughts and aspirations. Because of the confidence and trust fostered by this environment, the author felt free to take chances and follow their passions without worrying about criticism or failure.

Giving Motivating Role Models:

Dad was aware of how important role models are in developing an entrepreneurial mindset. He introduced the author to successful businessmen and entrepreneurs who had persevered and developed unique concepts. Dad demonstrated the opportunities and possible rewards of entrepreneurial endeavors by recounting tales of their travels. The author's ambition and desire to have a significant effect through their own entrepreneurial ventures were stoked by these role models, who provided as a source of inspiration.

Promotion of a Growth Mindset

Dad established in the author a growth attitude that stressed the value of ongoing education, perseverance, and accepting failure as a stepping stone to achievement. He pushed the author to see failure as a priceless learning opportunity and taught that obstacles and problems were chances for progress. A crucial quality for any prospective entrepreneur, Dad instilled in the author the endurance and resilience required to overcome challenges and recover from failures.

Promoting an Innovative and Creative Culture:

Dad encouraged the author to look outside the box and consider novel solutions by fostering a culture of invention and creativity. He encouraged a way of thinking that emphasized inquiry, experimentation, and the search for novel concepts. Dad frequently had illuminating conversations with the author, encouraging them to question the present quo and look for fresh solutions to issues. The author's desire to use entrepreneurship to effect significant change was stoked by this atmosphere of invention.

Establishing a business-oriented work ethic:

Dad emphasized the value of patience, dedication, and hard work when pursuing business objectives. He imposed high standards and demanded that they take responsibility of their efforts, which helped to instill in the author an entrepreneurial work ethic. Dad instilled in the author the concept of perseverance, instructing her to be tenacious in the face of difficulties and to uphold a strict work ethic even when achievement looked far off. This work ethic served as the cornerstone for the author's entrepreneurial activities, influencing their resolve and dedication to make ideas a reality.

Promoting Business Acumen and Financial Literacy:

Dad understood the value of business and financial knowledge in the entrepreneurial journey. He urged the author to gain a firm grasp of monetary concepts, budgeting, and strategic planning. Dad helped the author understand the foundations of business, such as market analysis, competitive positioning, and profit production. When it came to making judgments and creating viable business models, the author's financial literacy and business savvy proved to be excellent assets.

A person's perspective and objectives can be changed for the better by nurturing their entrepreneurial spirit. The author's perspective was significantly shaped by her father's support of entrepreneurship, which instilled in her an attitude that values creativity, independence, and pursuing one's passions. Dad created an environment where the author felt encouraged to seize entrepreneurial possibilities through a supportive environment, motivating role models, a growth mindset, a culture of creativity, an entrepreneurial work ethic, and a concentration on financial literacy and business acumen. Beyond their own accomplishments, the author's vision, resiliency, and ambition have all been shaped by this fostering. The ability to negotiate the complexity of the modern world, effect significant change, and embrace the endless opportunities that lie ahead is made possible by the cultivation of the entrepreneurial spirit.

Discuss how values play a part in managing and protecting a financial legacy in section 4.3, "Balancing Wealth and Values."

Money assets are only one aspect of wealth; it is also based on the values and tenets that govern its administration and preservation. A key component of leaving a lasting financial legacy is striking a balance between riches and values. This essay examines how values might be used to manage and protect a financial legacy. We seek to highlight the necessity of values-driven decision-making in wealth management by talking about the significance of integrating charity, fostering financial responsibility in future generations, and embracing sustainable investment strategies.

Integrating Personal Values with Wealth:

Making sure that financial choices and investments are in line with a person's fundamental principles and views is a key component of aligning money with personal values. It necessitates a thorough comprehension of one's values and a dedication to making decisions that are consistent with them. People give their financial activities a feeling of purpose and meaning by connecting riches with their personal values. The ability to make decisions that are in line with their ethical, social, and environmental values is made possible by this alignment, which encourages honesty and authenticity in wealth management.

Bringing Philanthropy Together:

Philanthropy is essential for striking a balance between values and money. It enables people to use their financial resources to support causes that are consistent with their values and have a good impact on society. Philanthropy can be included into wealth management so that people can address important societal concerns, help deserving causes, and leave a lasting legacy. As it enables people to change lives and advance society, philanthropy gives people a sense of fulfillment and purpose.

Future Generations' Financial Responsibility Development:

Future generations must be taught financial responsibility if a financial legacy is to be preserved. It is possible for parents and grandparents to guarantee that their wealth is handled intelligently and in accordance with their beliefs for future generations by providing values-based financial education to their children and grandkids. Fostering a sense of fiscal responsibility and stewardship through the teaching of budgeting, saving, investing, and giving back principles.

Future generations will be given the knowledge and abilities needed to successfully navigate the challenges of wealth management while upholding the family's values and legacy.

Promoting Family Governance and Open Communication:

In order to maintain a balance between wealth and values over generations, open communication and family governance are crucial. Families can develop a shared knowledge of their values, objectives, and aspirations by setting up a framework for open discussion and decision-making. Transparency, trust, and family cohesion are fostered via regular family gatherings, moderated talks, and the formulation of family values and mission declarations. Families are better equipped to make wise financial decisions that are consistent with their shared values thanks to open communication, which also helps to protect the family's financial heritage.

Using sustainable investing techniques:

A key element of striking a balance between money and values is the incorporation of sustainable investment methods into wealth management. When making investment decisions, sustainable investing means taking environmental, social, and governance (ESG) considerations into account. Individuals can match their investments with their ideals and foster change by adopting ESG criteria. Sustainable investment prioritizes

assisting businesses that place a high priority on ethics, social impact, and good governance. This strategy not only enables people to contribute positively to society but also aids in managing long-term financial possibilities and hazards.

Constructing a Multi-Dimensional Legacy

Financial considerations are only one aspect of balancing wealth and values. It entails creating a multifaceted legacy that includes not only material wealth but also immaterial resources like knowledge, experiences, relationships, and societal effect. People can leave a lasting impression on future generations by imparting their morals, knowledge, and lessons learned from experience. This multifaceted legacy makes sure that money is not only conserved but also used to improve the lives of people, communities, and society at large.

A key component of managing and preserving a financial legacy is striking a balance between riches and values. Individuals can build a financial legacy that reflects their priorities, values, and aspirations by integrating philanthropy, aligning wealth with personal values, encouraging open communication and family governance, and adopting sustainable investment practices. By doing this, people not only protect their riches but also leave a significant legacy that goes beyond material benefits. A person can manage their wealth with integrity, purpose, and a desire to making a positive influence in the world by choosing to balance their riches and values.

Chapter 5

Chapter 5:
Honoring Dad's Prosperity

We have a particular place in our hearts and lives for the wealth and achievement of our fathers. They support us and secure a better future for us by working nonstop to make ends meet. We shall examine the importance of celebrating our dads' success in this essay. We will examine how their perseverance, commitment, and successes affect our lives, how they affect our beliefs and goals, and the significance of showing our appreciation for their efforts. By reflecting on this experience, we hope to increase our gratitude for our fathers and recognize their contribution to our own success.

Body:

The Impact of Dad's Success on Our Lives

The wealth of our dads has an impact on many facets of our lives, molding us into the people we are now. They act as role models, fostering vital virtues like self-control, tenacity, and integrity. They give us a solid foundation via their labor of love, and they motivate us to pursue our own goals and desires. Dad's success has an impact on our emotional and psychological growth in addition to our material well-being. They establish an atmosphere that allows us to develop and bloom because of the stability and security they offer.

Observations from Dad's Success:

The success that our fathers have attained frequently comes with priceless lessons that we may take away and apply to our own lives. They instill in us the value of setting objectives, cultivating a solid work ethic, and viewing difficulties as chances for improvement. Dad's accomplishment shows us that failure is really a stepping stone on the path to achievement rather than the end. They provide knowledge garnered from their own experiences, assisting us in choosing wisely and overcoming challenges. Their triumphant tales encourage us to keep going in the face of difficulty because we know that success is possible with grit and fortitude.

How It Affects Our Values and Goals:

Our beliefs and aspirations are shaped by our fathers' success, which affects the directions we choose in life. We appreciate the value of education, professional development, and ongoing learning after seeing their successes. Dad's success inspires us to pursue excellence in our chosen professions because we know that perseverance and hard effort may produce similar results. Their success inspires us to have huge dreams and the self-assurance to go for them, which fuels our ambition and pushes us over our limits.

expressing gratitude for your father's success:

We must be sure to let our fathers know how much we appreciate their success. They have given up so much to take care of us and make sure we are okay. By recognizing their efforts, expressing gratitude for their dedication, and appreciating the influence they have had on our lives, we may honor dad's prosperity. This can be accomplished by expressing sincere thanks for their contributions and by engaging in modest actions of gratitude like spending time with them and showing interest in their successes. Another method to show our gratitude and recognize their prosperity is to celebrate their accomplishments.

Keeping the Legacy Alive:

Honoring dad's success also entails continuing the legacy they have created. We must uphold and build upon the accomplishments made by our predecessors, who sacrificed much to make life better for us. We may accomplish this by living up to the principles they taught us, working hard to achieve both personal and professional success, and taking care of our own families. Future generations can continue the cycle of wealth and be motivated to pursue their own goals by receiving the wisdom we received from our dads.

Honoring dad's success is a sign of how much of an influence our fathers have had on our lives. Our ideals, objectives, and personal development are shaped by their perseverance, commitment, and achievement. It is crucial to thank them for their contributions and to recognize their achievements. We ensure that their prosperity is passed on to succeeding generations by upholding their legacy and living by the principles they have taught us. Dads are the foundation of our families and the impetus for our personal success, so let's constantly remember and celebrate their success.

Dad's Success as an Inspirational Source:

The wealth of our fathers is a great source of motivation for us. We are inspired to strive for greatness by seeing how hard they work, how determined they are, and how resilient they are in achieving their goals. Dad's success serves as a constant inspiration that, with drive, tenacity, and the correct attitude, we can also overcome challenges and flourish in our own life. Their successes serve as a source of inspiration and hope for us, inspiring us to strive for excellence and go beyond our comfort zones.

Dad's Financial Success and Family Values:

The success of our fathers was not just measured in terms of money; it also included the ideals they instilled in us. Strong family values like love, unity, and support typically go hand in hand with dad's financial success. They instill in us the value of cherishing and cultivating our relationships, placing a high value on the welfare of our loved ones, and encouraging a feeling of community. Dad's success ends up serving as a symbol of the importance of family and how it affects our sense of fulfillment and general happiness.

Accepting Dad's Path to Prosperity

Every father's success has been the result of an individual and motivational path. It is critical to acknowledge and value the journey someone took to succeed. There may have been obstacles, disappointments, and sacrifices along Dad's journey. We can better appreciate the significance of their accomplishments if we recognize and comprehend their challenges. Accepting dad's path to success enables us to relate to their struggles, absorb their teachings, and cultivate resiliency and tenacity in our own life.

Supporting and Motivating Dad to Achieve Success:

Giving constant support and encouragement is one of the most heartfelt ways to celebrate dad's success. It is important for us to support our fathers in their continuous quest for prosperity, just as they have been there for us throughout our lives. Our support underlines their importance in our lives and shows our unshakable faith in their skills, whether it be by celebrating their new endeavors, providing words of encouragement during trying times, or simply being a listening ear.

Repaying the Favor:

It is crucial to understand the wider effects that affluence can have on society as we pay tribute to our ancestors' success. The accomplishment of Dad can spur good change not only in our families but even in our society. We may spread prosperity by passing on the knowledge, principles, and chances that have been given to us. We may improve people's lives by deeds of kindness, mentoring, and generosity, preserving the prosperity spirit and motivating future generations to fulfill their own aspirations.

Beyond merely praising their material well-being, dads should be honored for their prosperity. It entails accepting their journey, finding motivation in their successes, and cultivating an attitude of thankfulness and support. By celebrating our fathers' success, we not only recognize their accomplishments but also the significant impact they have had on our lives and the legacy they have left behind. As we carve out our own pathways to riches and have a positive impact on the world, let us keep their lessons, ideals, and goals close to our hearts.

THE FINANCIAL LEGACY

The Success of Dad as a Symbol of Sacrifice

Every successful father has a tale of sacrifice. Dad's success frequently comes at the expense of the numerous sacrifices they have made in order to ensure the present and future of their family. To make sure our needs were addressed, they might have put in long hours, gone through difficult times personally, or put their own aspirations on wait. Recognizing and appreciating the efforts they have done on our behalf is essential to honoring dad's prosperity. It acts as a motivator to commemorate their sacrifices by utilizing the opportunities they have given us to the fullest. It serves as a reminder of their devotion.

Dad's Financial Success and Support:

Although having a stable financial situation is important for dad's prosperity, they also offer important emotional support. When we face difficulties, our fathers are there to offer support, listen, and give us a sense of stability. They provide unwavering affection and assurance, and they are the rock we can rely on. Recognizing and returning their emotional support in our own lives is an important part of honoring dad's success. We maintain the tie of love and gratitude by being a source of support for them when they are weak.

Dad's Wealth as a Catalyst for Personal Development

Our fathers' fathers' success frequently throws open possibilities for our own personal development. Through their achievement, they give us access to knowledge, guidance, and tools that can advance us. Seizing these chances and making the most of the riches they've given us is paying tribute to dad's prosperity. In order to do this, we must embrace lifelong learning, pursue personal and professional growth, and work to realize our full potential. By making the most of the advantages we have been given, we pay tribute to the financial commitment our dad made to our future.

Dad's Prosperity Honored via Legacy Building

Dad's success serves as a reminder to us of the value of leaving a lasting and meaningful legacy. The accomplishments of our fathers paved the way for the legacy we will leave for future generations. Making decisions and acting in ways that have a positive influence on our neighborhoods, society, and the environment is part of paying tribute to dad's success.

It entails teaching our own children the same morals, work ethics, and sense of mission in order to motivate them to carry on prosperity. We respect the legacy our fathers have given to us by creating a legacy founded in integrity, compassion, and wealth.

Honoring Dad's Success as a Family:

Finally, a family celebration is one of the most enjoyable ways to acknowledge dad's success. The chance to join together and express thanks for the richness and benefits we have received is provided by gatherings, milestones, and accomplishments. We improve the connection within the family, make treasured memories, and increase the feeling of love and unity by jointly enjoying dad's financial success. These occasions serve as a reminder of the accomplishments and happiness our fathers have brought into our lives.

Honoring dad's success involves a variety of activities, such as acknowledging their sacrifices, offering emotional support, grabbing chances for personal development, leaving a lasting legacy, and celebrating their successes. It is a constant commitment to show our appreciation, return the love and support they have shown us, and make sure their prosperity lasts for many years. Because it is evidence of their unshakable commitment and the immense influence they have had on our lives, let us treasure and celebrate the prosperity of our fathers.

Highlighting the Non-Financial Aspects of Dad's Legacy: 5.1 Emotional Inheritance

Often, when we consider inheritance, we think about financial assets. But the legacy that our fathers leave behind is considerably broader than just material wealth. Equally important is emotional inheritance, which consists of morals, work ethics, and ties to the family. We shall examine the non-financial facets of dad's legacy and their significant influence on our lives in this essay. We will examine the morals and ethics they instill in us, their dedication to their jobs, and their promotion of close family ties. We may commemorate the legacy of our dads and pass them on to subsequent generations by acknowledging and appreciating these priceless gifts.

The Influence of Values

The set of values our fathers instill in us is one of the most important non-financial inheritances. The moral compass they impart in us, forming our character and directing our decisions, is Dad's legacy. Our guiding principles become things like honesty, integrity, empathy, and perseverance. Dad's emphasis on moral conduct instills in us the value of prioritizing doing what is right, even when it is difficult. These principles influence not just our social interactions but also how we live our personal lives, encouraging accountability and making a positive impact on the world.

Work ethics and tenacity:

The perseverance and hard ethic they exhibit throughout their lives are part of their father's legacy. We can learn the value of hard effort, discipline, and perseverance by watching how dedicated and committed they are to their careers. Dad's work ethic instills in us the idea that success is something we must work for and be willing to face challenges in order to achieve. Their tenacity in the face of difficulties inspires us to persevere in our own endeavors and serves as a reminder that failures are only chances for improvement.

Fostering Family Ties

Dad's legacy is firmly based on the relationships of the family. Our fathers are essential in fostering these ties and giving our families a sense of unity, love, and support. The amount of time they spend together, the traditions they keep, and the happy and humorous times they have together will be Dad's legacy. They show us the value of valuing family, building solid relationships, and developing an environment where everyone feels valued and respected by their presence and activity. These ties to our families grow stronger, more comfortable, and more stable over time.

Providing leadership examples:

The leadership they display is another facet of dad's legacy. Our fathers serve as examples, exhibiting strong leadership abilities and traits. Dad's leadership affects how we approach tasks and negotiate relationships, whether it is in the home, the workplace, or the community. They instill in us the value of honesty, compassion, and the capacity to uplift and empower others. Dad's leadership legacy inspires us to assume leadership roles and have a positive influence in our own spheres of influence.

Wisdom Transmission:

The wisdom they pass on to us through their experiences and life lessons is another way they carry on Dad's legacy. Their advice turns into a useful tool while we go on our own. Dad's advice covers a wide range of topics, such as interpersonal interactions, decision-making, and personal development. They provide insightful advice based on their own triumphs, setbacks, and difficulties. Dad gives us the information and direction we need to make wise decisions, avoid mistakes, and lead satisfying lives by passing on their wisdom.

Resilience training:

One essential quality that dad left behind is resilience. Life is full of ups and downs, and our fathers instill in us the value of overcoming hardship. Dad's tenacity is evident in the way his children respond to setbacks, surmount challenges, and grow stronger as a result of challenging circumstances. They instruct us to consider setbacks and failures as chances for development and learning rather than letting them discourage us. Dad left us with the self-assurance and resolve required to meet life's obstacles head-on with courage and tenacity.

Promotion of Self-Reflection

Another part of Dad's legacy is to promote introspection and personal development. They instruct us to reflect, assess our decisions, and make an effort to better ourselves. Dad guides us in becoming self-aware, identifying our talents and areas for improvement. They inspire us to make plans, follow our passions, and work tirelessly to advance both personally and professionally. A lifelong commitment to progress is fostered by Dad's legacy of self-reflection, ensuring that we are continuously improving and becoming the best versions of ourselves.

Enhancing Emotional health

A crucial component of dad's legacy is emotional health. Our fathers are crucial in fostering emotional well-being within the family. They support open communication, empathy, and emotional expression. Dad left us with the gift of a secure place where we can openly discuss our joys, anxieties, and difficulties without fear of being judged. Dad gives us the skills to manage the intricacies of life, form enduring relationships, and become resilient in the face of hardship through supporting our emotional wellbeing.

Spreading compassion and kindness

The impact of Dad goes beyond our immediate family. They encourage us to show compassion and kindness to others. Dad instills in us the value of compassion, charity, and contributing to society. They show the value of helping people in need by their deeds of kindness and participation in philanthropic activities. Dad's legacy of kindness inspires us to improve the lives of others, starting a kindness chain reaction that spreads far beyond our own lives.

Dad's non-financial legacies that significantly influence our life fall under the category of emotional inheritance. Our fathers' beliefs, work ethic, sense of family, leadership abilities, knowledge, fortitude, and emotional stability become compass points for our own journeys. We preserve and transmit the essence of our fathers' legacy to subsequent generations by recognizing and valuing these priceless gifts. The non-monetary components of dad's legacy should be treasured and honored since they serve as the basis for our moral character, interpersonal connections, and potential for good global impact.

Encouragement of a Sense of Responsibility

Dad left us with the burden of instilling accountability in us. They help us learn to take responsibility for our deeds, accept responsibility for our decisions, and carry out our responsibilities. Because of Dad's emphasis on accountability, we have a strong work ethic and a will to keep our promises. We improve ourselves, our families, and society as a whole by accepting responsibility for our words and deeds. Dad's legacy of responsibility becomes a tenet that guides our behavior and determines how we affect the world.

Educating for Education Value:

Dad's legacy is critically dependent on education. Our fathers are aware of the importance of education and how it may change people's lives. They stress the importance of education, both official and informal, and encourage us to continue learning throughout our lives. Dad left us with a legacy of education that inspires us to learn more, extend our views, and constantly strive for intellectual and personal development. They give us the skills to adapt to a world that is changing quickly and enable us to make wise decisions by instilling this value in us.

fostering equilibrium and wellbeing

Dad left us with the responsibility of encouraging harmony and wellbeing in our lives. They instill in us the value of caring for our physical and emotional well-being. Dad encourages us to strike a healthy balance between our career, family, and personal interests. They place a strong emphasis on the value of self-care, stress reduction, and upholding sound boundaries. Dad's legacy of encouraging harmony and wellbeing serves as a gentle reminder to value our health, cherish our relationships, and discover happiness and fulfillment in all facets of life.

Developing an Attitude of Gratitude

The profound quality of gratitude is an inheritance from my dad. Our fathers instill in us the value of acknowledging both the major and minor blessings in our life. Dad's emphasis on gratitude inspires us to show our appreciation for others, recognise their efforts and sacrifices, and develop a positive outlook. We gain a greater understanding of life and the relationships we value by practicing thankfulness. Dad's legacy of thankfulness enables us to enjoy the present, foster meaningful relationships, and inspire others around us.

Development of Independence

Dad left us with a strong sense of independence. Our fathers recognize the value of giving us the knowledge and assurance to live independently. They encourage individuality and self-reliance while simultaneously offering direction and assistance. Our ability to make decisions, take calculated chances, and face obstacles with confidence is a result of Dad's legacy of encouraging independence. Dad encourages independence in us so that we can be ready for the responsibilities and opportunities that lie ahead and live happy, purposeful lives.

Transferring Family Traditions:

The legacy that my dad leaves behind includes our family customs. They give us a sense of continuity, our roots, and family ties are strengthened. Dad transmits beloved customs that have been passed down over the centuries. These traditions have significant significance and foster a sense of identity and belonging, whether they involve commemorating festivals, eating together, or taking part in certain activities.

We are able to connect with our heritage, make enduring memories, and transmit the richness of our family's history to the next generation because to Dad's legacy of family customs.

Dad's legacy intangibles have tremendous worth in forming our personalities, interpersonal connections, and general wellbeing. Our fathers have a profound influence on our lives through the values they establish, the work ethic they demonstrate, and the strong familial ties they foster. We make sure that dad's legacy of non-financial components continues to impact and inspire us and future generations by recognizing, acknowledging, and passing on these priceless talents. Let's embrace and honor the enormous value of the non-material facets of dad's legacy since they serve as the cornerstones for our families' resiliency, strength, and love.

Sharing personal anecdotes and stories that illustrate the ideals Dad instilled and how the author continues to uphold them constitutes section 5.2, "Honoring Dad's values."

Our character is shaped by and our decisions are influenced by our father's values. They are an expression of his viewpoints, his life, and the teachings he teaches. In this essay, we will look at individual experiences and tales that serve as examples of the principles our dads taught us. We will explore how these principles have affected our lives and how we uphold them now. These stories provide as evidence of dad's principles' significant influence and demonstrate their enduring legacy.

Value: Integrity

The value of being honest in all facets of life was something that Dad always emphasized. He thought that relationships are strengthened and trust is built through honesty. When I was in school, I once felt tempted to cheat on a test. I knew that integrity was the most important thing to him, therefore I couldn't bring myself to give in to temptation. Instead, I choose to diligently study and received a mark that was below what I had hoped for. However, any little disappointment was greatly overshadowed by the gratification of knowing that I had upheld my father's principles. I still uphold my father's devotion to honesty by acting in accordance with my morals in both my personal and professional activities.

Value: Generosity

Dad emphasized kindness as a fundamental principle. He showed me the power of kindness and how it can change people's lives. In the past, on a chilly winter night, we saw a homeless individual attempting to find shelter. Dad came to a stop and started talking to the

genuine empathy and concern for the other person. He continued by offering his coat and some hot meals. This wonderful deed made a lasting impression on me. By helping out at nearby shelters and performing random acts of kindness wherever I can, I try to uphold my father's value of kindness today. Dad's conviction that compassion has the ability to change people's lives continues to motivate me to improve the lives of others.

Value: Resilience

Dad's unshakeable faith in the ability of tenacity has had a significant influence on my life. He showed me that failures and setbacks are just stepping stones on the path to achievement. I can recall a period when I experienced a major career setback. I was so saddened that I thought about giving up. Dad, on the other hand, emphasized to me that success is instead measured by one's capacity to rise above setbacks and continue on. He inspired me to persevere by sharing his own stories of overcoming obstacles. I was motivated to continue working toward my ambitions by my dad's tenacity. Today, I carry on my father's legacy of tenacity by continuing to fight through difficulties.

Value: Compassion

My father's empathy taught me the value of comprehending and relating to people. I can well remember a time when I was grieving intensely over a personal loss. Dad simply listened while sitting next to me and holding my hand. He provided his presence and empathy instead of attempting to ease the suffering or provide counsel. I learned the value of compassion from that event, and I also gained a deeper comprehension of what it is to be human. By actively listening to people, providing encouragement, and attempting to understand other viewpoints, I pay tribute to my father's value of empathy today. I'm continually motivated by my father's capacity for empathy to develop deep relationships and have a positive impact on the world.

Respect is a value

Dad taught respect as a fundamental virtue in our household. He valued respecting people's differences of opinion and treating them with decency. I recall a family get-together where there was a contentious debate about a particular subject. Dad made sure that everyone's voice was heard and encouraged courteous discussion despite divergent viewpoints. He set an example of courteous conduct by attentively listening, accepting opposing ideas, and remaining polite. By valuing diversity, encouraging open dialogue, and treating others with kindness and understanding, I pay tribute to my father's value of respect today. My interactions and relationships are still shaped by my dad's dedication to respect.

Value: Kindness

My father's generosity taught me the virtue of sharing with others and the joy of giving. We once worked together as volunteers at a neighborhood charity event, as I recall. Dad committed his time and money to helping those in need, and he inspired me to follow in his footsteps. His act of selflessness and the effect it had on others inspired me to live with a purpose. I continue to uphold my father's example of generosity by giving to charitable organizations, giving back to my community, and being as kind as I can be. My father's kindness has always motivated me to improve people's lives.

Value: Stubbornness

Dad instilled in me the virtue of perseverance and determination in accomplishing my goals. I can still picture the summer I made the decision to launch a side hustle. Dad encouraged me to follow my entrepreneurial drive and served as my strongest supporter. He helped me overcome the obstacles, motivated me to put in a lot of effort, and acknowledged my successes. His own commitment to hard work provided as a continual reminder of the benefits of making an attempt. By tackling my undertakings with tenacity and a strong work ethic today, I pay tribute to my father's belief in the worth of hard labor. Dad's dedication to working hard inspires me to pursue greatness in whatever I do.

The stories and personal anecdotes mentioned above provide us a glimpse of the principles our fathers instilled in us and the ways we now uphold those principles. Dad's values act as guiding principles that mold our character and direct our activities, whether they are honesty, kindness, perseverance, empathy, respect, generosity, or hard work. By passing on these principles, we not only respect the legacy of our dads but also have a good influence on the world. Dad instilled ideals in us, and we should respect and honor them because they are lifelong gifts that have shaped our lives and motivated us to be the greatest versions of ourselves.

5.3 Paying it forward: Talk about the author's dedication to ensuring that future generations continue Dad's financial legacy.

Dad's financial legacy involves more than just amassing riches; it also involves the need to entrust his knowledge and assets to succeeding generations. The author's dedication to passing on his financial legacy to the next generation by making sure it is protected will be discussed in this article.

We'll talk about the value of fostering a charitable mindset, prudent money management, and financial education. By respecting dad's financial legacy and giving the following generations the resources and information they require, we can enable them to make wise decisions, establish financial stability, and have a beneficial impact on their neighborhoods.

Financial Literacy

Providing future generations with financial education is an essential part of carrying on dad's financial legacy. Dad gave us the information and tools to make wise financial decisions because he recognized the value of financial literacy. We are now accountable for continuing this promise. We give our children and grandchildren the tools they need to successfully navigate the intricacies of the financial world by educating them about budgeting, saving, investing, and managing debt. We make sure students have a strong foundation for financial success through open dialogue and useful teachings.

prudence in wealth management

Dad left behind a sound financial foundation as well as a dedication to prudent wealth management. He underlined the value of good financial planning, which includes setting aside money for investments and creating an estate plan. Future generations are taught the need of fiscal responsibility and long-term financial planning as we pass on dad's financial legacy to them. We advise them to prioritize saving, diversify their holdings, and build long-term wealth. We enable future generations to make wise financial decisions and ensure their financial future by passing down these ideas.

Giving back and philanthropy:

Dad's financial legacy includes a dedication to philanthropy and giving back to society in addition to the accumulation of money for personal gain. Dad instilled in us a charitable perspective because he recognized the value in having a positive impact on the world. By transferring dad's financial legacy, we make sure that subsequent generations continue to be generous and philanthropic. We cultivate a culture of giving that goes well beyond our own lifetimes by involving our children and grandkids in charity initiatives, instilling in them the value of social responsibility, and encouraging them to support issues they are passionate about.

Mentoring and direction:

Giving dad's financial legacy to your children requires more than simply giving them money; it also requires coaching and guiding them. We take on the responsibility of assisting future generations in their financial travels, just as dad acted as a mentor to us. We provide help as they negotiate the difficulties of wealth management and financial decision-making by sharing our experiences, giving guidance, and sharing our knowledge. By being a dependable source and sharing our knowledge, we enable clients to make wise decisions and stay clear of typical mistakes. We make sure that dad's financial legacy is preserved through mentoring and enhanced by the combined wisdom and experiences of each generation.

Encouragement of Innovation and Entrepreneurship

Dad's financial legacy might also include an innovative and entrepreneurial drive. Dad may have been an entrepreneur himself or appreciated the prospects offered by such ventures.

We inspire future generations to pursue their business ambitions and embrace innovation as we pass on dad's financial legacy. We give them the assistance, direction, and tools they require in order to realize their business aspirations. We enable people to write their own financial success stories, contribute to economic progress, and innovate by encouraging an entrepreneurial mindset.

Financial Management:

THE FINANCIAL LEGACY

Leaving dad's financial legacy entails teaching future generations the importance of fiscal responsibility. Dad was aware of the significance of resource management and sound financial judgment. By educating future generations on the value of prudent financial management, we carry on this tradition. We stress the significance of striking a balance between financial objectives, moral considerations, and environmentally sound activities. We make sure that dad's financial legacy is in line with the principles of the future by promoting mindful consumption, environmental awareness, and socially responsible investing.

A noble obligation that calls for a dedication to financial education, prudent wealth management, giving, mentoring, and promoting entrepreneurship is leaving dad's financial legacy to future generations. We enable future generations to make wise financial decisions, establish financial security, and have a positive impact on their communities by instilling these principles and providing them with the knowledge and skills they require. By passing it on, we make sure that dad's financial legacy survives and continues to spur social and individual development. Let's take on this duty with commitment and kindness, respecting dad's financial legacy and building a better future for future generations.

Financial Independence Encouragement:

It's crucial to promote financial independence in future generations as we pass dad's financial legacy on. Dad recognized the importance of independence and the power that comes with financial independence. We stress the value of creating financial objectives, adhering to a budget, and making wise financial decisions to our children and grandchildren. By fostering a feeling of financial independence in them, we provide them the knowledge and abilities they need to manage their own finances and come to decisions that are consistent with their goals and values.

The Value of Delayed Gratification is Taught:

The value of delaying gratification was one of the important lessons my father taught me. He realized that perseverance and discipline are frequently needed for financial success. We emphasize the importance of saving for the future and making sensible financial decisions in the present as we pass along dad's financial legacy. We impart to the next generation the benefits of postponing short-term demands in favor of long-term financial security. We can ensure that future generations can create a solid foundation for their financial security by developing the practice of delaying pleasure.

How to Develop a Growth Mindset

Dad's financial legacy must be passed down while also encouraging future generations to view challenges as opportunities. Dad was a firm believer in the benefits of perseverance, flexibility, and lifelong learning. We urge our kids and grandkids to take on challenges, learn from mistakes, and develop a mindset that sees failures as chances to improve.

By encouraging a growth mentality, we provide the resilience and adaptability necessary for future generations to successfully navigate the constantly shifting financial landscape and seize opportunities for financial success.

Putting a Focus on Ethical Investing

Dad's financial legacy includes a dedication to ethical investing in addition to his material fortune. We impart to the next generation the value of matching their investments with their values and the potential effects that their financial decisions may have on the environment and society. By educating them about impact investing, sustainable investing, and socially responsible investing, we enable them to make financial decisions that not only produce returns but also help to improve the world. Dad's example of ethical investing serves as a reminder that achieving financial success and having a significant impact are not mutually exclusive.

Maintaining Family Values

Saving family values is just as important as transferring riches when it comes to carrying on dad's financial legacy. We make sure that the ideals and concepts that underlie dad's financial success are understood by future generations. We talk about our family's history, our problems and victories, and the principles that helped dad make sound financial decisions. By conserving and transmitting these family values, we give the next generation a solid moral compass to guide them through their financial life and make sure that dad's financial legacy continues to be rooted in values that transcend just materialistic considerations.

Making a Financial Empowerment Legacy:

The goal of leaving dad's financial legacy is to empower future generations financially. The goal is to provide the next generation with the information, know-how, and resources they need to manage their money wisely, pursue their goals, and improve the lives of others. By equipping people with financial literacy, ethical wealth management techniques, and a charitable mindset, we have an impact that lasts well past our own lives. Dad's financial legacy acts as a catalyst for change, encouraging subsequent generations to create their own financial empowerment legacies and having a long-lasting effect on the globe.

Financial education, responsible asset management, philanthropy, independence, delayed gratification, a growth mentality, ethical investing, the preservation of family values, and financial empowerment are just a few of the many aspects of passing on dad's financial legacy to future generations. By embracing these facets, we guarantee that dad's financial legacy lives on and continues to be a compass for future generations. Let's approach this duty with purpose, kindness, and a determination to provide our families and communities a better financial future.

www.ingramcontent.com/pod-product-compliance
Lightning Source LLC
LaVergne TN
LVHW020427080526
838202LV00055B/5066